*Loving
Memory*

Loving Memory

ISHMAEL

Reflections on Pain and Death

WORD PUBLISHING
Nelson Word Ltd
Milton Keynes, England

WORD AUSTRALIA
Kilsyth, Australia

STRUIK CHRISTIAN BOOKS (PTY) LTD
Cape Town, South Africa

JOINT DISTRIBUTORS SINGAPORE–
ALBY COMMERCIAL ENTERPRISES LTD
and
CAMPUS CRUSADE ASIA LTD

PHILIPPINE CAMPUS CRUSADE FOR CHRIST
Quezon City, Philippines

CHRISTIAN MARKETING NEW ZEALAND LTD
Havelock North, New Zealand

JENSCO LTD
Hong Kong

SALVATION BOOK CENTRE
Malaysia

LOVING MEMORY

Dedicated to William John Smale for all the loving memories that you have given to your wife Dorothy, to your children and their partners, Tim and Gill, Heather and David, Ian and Irene and to your grandchildren Joshua, Laura, Rebecca, Sarah, Anna, Jon, Ben, Suzy, Daniel and Joseph.

All royalties for this book will go to Mum.

Contents

Father and Son

Getting old is a strange process. Each glance in the mirror reveals more grey hairs on your head and even more grey hairs finding their final destination either tangled up in a comb or blocking the drainage hole in the bath or the shower.

The ever-expanding waistline is another telltale sign that the body, owing to its natural ageing process, is not managing to burn up the same amount of energy as it did a few years ago. It follows that most Christians, contrary to obeying the words of Jesus and 'taking no thought for what we should eat and drink', become totally obsessed and live with one eye examining the numbers written before the letters 'k cal' on every food product they buy, and the other eye weeping over numbers that appear as they stand on that most depressing invention known to man—the bathroom scales.

But our mind is another matter. As it sits proudly inside the round object resting on two broad shoulders, it remains totally oblivious to the number of years that our legs have had to carry it, and the heavy mass beneath it, around.

It still keeps informing us that we are not too old to

play football, race against other parents who are half our age at the school sports day, and charge up and down stairs all day long. It's not until our body screams 'I've had enough!' and collapses exhausted into a sad heap, that our mind also gets the depressing message that it's not as young as it used to be. In fact—although it never wants to face up to it—it too is getting old.

How we see ourselves is one story, but how we see others is not just another story, it's another book.

This book is about parents—my parents—and more specifically, my father . . .

Now here is something that you may never have thought about. Our parents, whom some of us love dearly and see fairly regularly, when they reach a certain time of life, seem to stop ageing. Let me explain.

Have you noticed how their hair, sometimes aided by a little artificial dye, stays the same colour, and however little or much has survived the years and is still on their head, now never alters. Nobody notices if they get fatter, as their height and weight has long since been established and become very much part of the character we love so much. So long as they remain mobile and reasonably healthy it seems to us that this is the way they always have been and always will be.

Mind you, they sometimes try to surprise us by opening up one of their many photograph albums. They then try to convince us that this photo is how they looked in their heyday when they were in their twenties, and we were such beautifully polite, well-behaved little children. Yes, they may have been good-looking in those days, but because we cannot remember them looking like that, these are not really our parents—our parents have always looked like the people who are showing us the photographs.

I praise God for the parents He gave me and that I have always been very close to them. I am also so grateful to God that I have always had a very special friendship with my father.

He was a typical parent, I guess, who in my eyes had looked and acted the same for as long as I had known him—which was all my life.

He still had hair on his head, though it had receded over the years, a waistline that showed he was very contented, rosy cheeks, a smiley face and a boyish sense of humour, which was the only characteristic that had not matured as the years had rolled on. It has been commented on more than one occasion that when he and I stood together, we looked and acted like brothers, which thrilled him more than yours truly, being twenty-seven years his junior!

Having stood the test of time, he has proved to be a loving and faithful husband to my mother Dorothy, and a generous and caring father to my sister Heather, brother Tim and me.

He was also very active in all areas of life.

Many years ago he had been the leading elder sent out to plant the church in which I now happen to be one of the elders. Years later, whilst in his sixties, he successfully headed up another church-plant in a different area of our locality. To say that he was sold out for God now seems like a bit of an understatement! I could see that his main aim in life was to serve Jesus and to be more like Him; and being a man of very little pride even in those later years of life, there was no task so menial or humbling that he would not joyfully do it if asked.

It seems so strange therefore that the vast majority of prophecies we are hearing today are saying that our future revival will be laid at the feet of our younger ones. Maybe it will. Maybe it won't. I for one would always encourage the young with all their youthful energy and exuberance. But the Church cannot afford to lose the maturity, experience, giftings and ministries that our more senior members have to contribute.

My father was also a very busy person. I've never heard him use the word 'bored' unless in connection with a tedious film or an overlong sermon. If he wasn't doing church work, he would either be sweating over the soil (he loved gardening), smacking snooker balls around a table, unsuccessfully fishing for fish (fortunately he had more luck with men), or fixing up his caravan ready for his next holiday which was probably six months away. I must tell you, he was a fanatic about preparation. He would spend more days loading his car and checking his caravan than he would actually holidaying.

Some may think that life begins at 65 and retirement, but with my father that certainly was not so. Although after retiring he discovered he had more time to do some of the things that he had previously pushed to the bottom of the list of priorities, he had never lived any of the previous 64 years waiting and longing for this time to come. He seemed to see every day as packed full of opportunity to serve God and have fun whilst doing so.

The old adage 'like father, like son' was true in some ways but not in others. I was more like a little chip off the old block. On the down side we shared similar temptations and distractions which we would discuss and pray about, fearing they had come through some dodgy ancestor and not wanting them to pass on to the next generation. On the up side we shared many similar interests and thrills in life and enjoyed pursuing them together.

But not all of Dad was passed on in my genes. We were quite opposite in many ways. Dad was tidy to the point of fussiness—I was untidy to the point of perfection. Dad, as I mentioned, loved his garden— mine was just a great big field that I would have covered in tarmac given half the chance. The biggest difference, however, was that Dad would rarely argue, and would prefer to remain quiet after putting over his perspective very clearly, whilst I was more like my mother who really enjoyed a good chat and would argue about anything. I may not always have had the

15

last word, but I would always have the most words to say.

From this close relationship you can see what a major influence and encouragement he was to me and the ministry that the Lord had given me.

He would studiously read through each book that I wrote, giving me very honest comments about his viewpoint on its content.

He would listen to all the hundreds of songs that I had written, again identifying clearly the ones he enjoyed and the ones that 'didn't do anything for him'.

He would listen to the numerous recordings I had made, making sure that I understood that his favourite tracks would always be the ones on which the children were not singing. This was not because he didn't like children—he just didn't like children singing.

He would sit, for what must have seemed like hours, and watch the videos I had recorded with my camcorder as I visited many different countries. He would humorously comment 'and here's me' every time my face appeared on the screen, blocking whatever beautiful scenery I happened to be standing in front of.

And finally, at least once a year, he would drive hundreds of miles to be alongside me—to encourage me, yet also to keep an eye on what I was doing. Whether I was at home or away, I always knew where to find him when I needed him. And it's as I write this that I now realise how much I *did* need him, which really is where my story begins . . .

Ups and Downs

Fathers are usually older than their children, but now came a time in my life where it seemed as if I was catching him up . . . rapidly!

In three days' time I was going to reach the age that most people seem to dread reaching—yes, 'the big four 0'.

Irene, my wonderful wife, had tried to soften the blow and play it down a little by arranging a massive party in a hotel. She had then made out a list of names of people who had been an influence in my life over that vast expanse of time, and invited them to come and celebrate this 'monumental' occasion with me.

In no time at all Irene's organisational skills had borne fruit. The RSVPs had all been RSVP'd, the catering had been catered for, and the live music arranged.

As well as marking the four decades that I had been inhabiting this planet, there was another reason for celebration. Twenty years before a much younger, slimmer and more good-looking Ishmael had started travelling up and down the country singing songs and telling people about Jesus. It was a great opportunity to show gratitude to all the wonderful guests, and even more to give thanks to Jesus.

Over these years, I must have worn out numerous cars and vans, and travelled thousands of miles. I am so grateful to God who has protected me on every journey.

Anyway, it was supper time and three days before the big event. Everything was so well organised and smooth running that nothing could possibly go wrong. Then the phone rang.

It was my mother, sounding very shaken and upset. She asked if I could get round to her house as quickly as possible, as something had happened to Dad.

Now my mother's a very stable lady and not given to panic. I was shocked by the sound of her voice and even more by what she was saying. How could anything happen to Dad? He was invincible. He'd been a war hero, survived massive injuries when a land mine hit him, lived miraculously with a piece of shrapnel the size of a ball-bearing right next to his brain for over forty years. What was Mum talking about—'Something's happened to Dad'?

My parents' house was only a few minutes away, so David (my sister Heather's husband) and I rushed round.

As we entered the garden I couldn't believe my eyes. Alongside the closely cut lawn was a wooden chalet. As it faced south, Dad and Mum spent many happy afternoons sitting inside it soaking up the sun. But this was no such occasion. It looked as if Dad had been up the ladder trying to repair the roof, and for some reason the ladder had given way and he had fallen straight onto the concrete underneath.

I ran over to Dad and stared at him. He had obviously been unconscious and was now in a state of semi-consciousness. His face was covered in blood and he was not talking any sense. The only audible word that I could decipher was 'sorry'. I couldn't believe it. He was actually apologising for the inconvenience he was causing us. I had never seen him like this before, and for the first time I realised that he was quite old, and often quite old people don't live through the shock of an accident like this. I didn't want to think the worst, but looking at his appearance and hearing his incoherency, I wondered if he was dying.

Mum had now calmed down, which I'm sure was no thanks to me. I just stood staring in unbelief at my father. David on the other hand was an ex-ambulance driver and seemed to know just what to do.

I assumed as he calmly took control of the situation that he had done this sort of thing many times before, yet I thought this must be different for him—being confronted with a loved one in this position.

We gently lifted Dad up and put him in the back of David's car. Whilst David and Mum sat in the front seat I sat in the back, and with a sense of necessity, held my still semi-conscious father close to me in a way that I had never held him before.

Of course, as father and son we had hugged each other before, but it was always in a polite greeting, dare I say even in an awkward, embarrassed sort of way, because it did not seem the normal thing that men do to each other. But now it was different. I hugged him and didn't want to let him go.

I must confess I am not a great one at putting my emotions into words, and I would have found it impossible to just speak to my Dad and tell him how much I appreciated and loved him. But now, as he felt me embracing him, I was hoping that maybe for the first time he could sense my deep feeling for him. I didn't want to lose him. I didn't want him to die.

I have never been very good at facing up to situations when anyone who is close to me is suffering. It's not that I lack compassion—it's just that I find it hard to cope with, especially if they are still in the same state after I have prayed for them. With Dad now sitting here next to me, I also discovered that it's not very easy to pray for loved ones in times of extreme emergency. I am a keen believer in the supernatural healing power of the Lord Jesus, and have had the privilege of praying for hundreds of people and seeing many of them instantly healed. But this was different. As I hugged his pain-filled body and looked at the face of the one who meant so much to me—a face now covered in blood—my emotions were so mixed up that I knew the words I was praying were coming from a heart with very little faith.

Praise God for the wonderful gift of speaking in tongues. For once I had nothing to say in English. I just felt useless, so I prayed over him in the supernatural language that God has given me, allowing the Holy Spirit inside me to do the praying for me. My mother and David were doing the same.

Dad had also always been a keen believer in the supernatural power of the Holy Spirit. He had always made it clear to all of us that it was only the Lord and the power of prayer that allowed him to be alive, since the shrapnel in his head, humanly speaking, should have killed him a long time ago.

The journey to the hospital seemed to last for ever. (They always do, don't they?) So, still with my arms firmly around Dad's body, I urged him to start speaking in tongues too. That's one thing that Dad never needed a lot of persuading to do. He loved speaking in tongues, whether in private praise or in a message for the whole of our church to hear.

Now, as he lay in pain in the back of the car, was no exception. Immediately his mouth was open and he started praising God. It was then, as I looked at him, that I wondered if praising God this way had to any degree quelled the pain. That's one of the many questions that I wish I had remembered to ask him.

After what seemed like an eternity we arrived at the hospital and Dad was put on a stretcher and taken into the casualty department. Again the praying and waiting continued, and finally he was taken away from us and put in a hospital ward.

Dad remained in the hospital for various check-ups, and during that time he had his wounds treated. How seriously was he injured? I guess we will never know, because we will never know what God healed whilst we were praying in the back of that car. I remain totally convinced that our prayers were heard and answered. We had so much to praise God for. Dad was still alive and improving rapidly.

As my big day arrived I had mixed feelings. Great excitement at the thought of meeting a lot of close friends, and great disappointment that Dad, one of my major inspirations, although released from hospital would be unlikely to be well enough to attend. The party was being held many miles from his house and I was sure that he would need to be at home resting as he was still in pain.

But—you guessed it! Dad wouldn't let his son down on such a big occasion. He entered the hotel, with his battered face and big smile, to the delight of everyone there, and he managed to stay for thirty minutes before beginning the long drive home. He slept the whole way.

His diary reads: 'I went for half an hour, which was enough for me, but I would really have liked to be there for all the time.'

My father had no time to think about himself. You see he spent all of his time thinking about others.

3

Heart and Soul

T he incidents surrounding the ladder accident changed quite a few things in my life.

For the first time I realised that my father was vulnerable. Not only could he suffer pain, but at any time he could be taken away from us altogether. I also felt a new bond between us and, dare I say it, even that a new and different relationship had been formed.

Up until now he had been my father and I his son. He told me what to do and for the most part, unless I felt particularly rebellious, I obeyed. If I needed any sort of help, I knew I could go to him and be assured of a listening ear and a generous heart. In fact things had not really changed much from when I was a tiny baby in a cot. When I called, he would be there.

But now, for the first time, things were starting to be reversed. For the first time I realised that he needed me.

After the party I remember approaching him and firmly laying down my rules for his survival. It was the first time that I had ever spoken to him in this way.

I banned him from climbing ladders and said that if ever he needed anything done on roofs again, he must call on David, my younger brother Tim, or even myself—and we would do whatever needed doing.

He realised how much he had scared his family, so he humbly submitted himself to my instructions. Even as I spoke though, I could imagine him chuckling to himself, knowing full well that the one who was now giving him orders was probably the least practical person he had ever met, and he knew that I would be more likely to fall through the roof than repair it!

But guessing what he was thinking did not deter me from continuing my flow and treating him like a naughty schoolboy. I threatened to take his ladder away from him and not let him have it back, if I ever heard of him going up it again.

Completely over-the-top stuff of course, but he knew me well enough to know that the son he'd trained up was invariably over the top. He was also well aware that it was coming from a heart that wanted the best for him.

Both my parents thoroughly enjoyed going to a large annual Christian event called Spring Harvest. This was always a unique and very special occasion, when about 9,000 people of a similar persuasion met together to praise God and learn about Jesus.

For many years Irene and I had been responsible for spending approximately six hours a day with what could be up to 900 eight- to eleven-year-olds. We called our meetings 'The Glorie Company', because as well as a lot of teaching and training, we also had a lot of praise, worship and fun.

Dad loved to be a part of all this, and was always dropping in at the end of our sessions to see what we were doing and, more importantly, what God was doing.

But more than being just an observer, he actually took an active role by adopting the personality of 'Grandpa Glorie'. Now this was great fun for the children, because they were informed that each afternoon Grandpa Glorie would be walking around the site. Furthermore, if they recognised him and got his autograph, they would get points for their team that evening. Each afternoon Dad would obediently pace around the enormous site, with his white Glorie hat on his head and his pen at the ready, and be mobbed by dozens of children rushing up to him screaming, 'Grandpa Glorie, can you give us your signature?', upon which he happily obliged.

It was now about a year and a half since the ladder accident, and all Dad's aches and pains had long since gone. He was in great shape. Being Easter, it was Spring Harvest time again, and my family had driven up to the Butlin's holiday camp in a town called Pwllheli in North Wales.

I remember looking at a map and thinking that the distance between Sussex, where we live, and Pwllheli didn't seem that far. But when we drove there, it seemed as if it would have been quicker to drive to the end of the earth. The only consolation was the beautiful scenery; but by the time we reached that, it was too dark to see it!

Dad decided he would come to the event too, but he was not content to drive directly there. He never seemed content to drive directly anywhere! He had a reputation for making a fifty-mile detour to stop at a favourite little coffee shop or some pub where he knew he would get a good meal.

This trip to north-west Wales was no different. En route (or more accurately, off route) he dropped into Dorset to visit Heather and David who were holidaying there. Then he drove to Builth Wells in mid-Wales to visit some friends and eventually reached his destination of Pwllheli. Of course this trip was not all in one day, but it certainly meant him doing a massive amount of driving in a short space of time—which I hasten to add he thoroughly enjoyed.

He arrived on the Saturday and really enjoyed attending the leaders' seminars that were organised throughout this Sunday. But he did mention that he felt a slight tightness across his chest.

On Monday morning as he and Mum were walking to the restaurant to get their breakfast—which was always one of his favourite meals of the day—he felt as if he had a touch of indigestion. He said he thought he would give breakfast a miss and go back to the chalet to lie down for a while. Although my Mother tried to insist that she go back with him, he would not hear of it, and told her to go on and eat as he would soon be all right.

Mum would not argue with Dad, not because she was a woman in total submission, but because she knew that he would feel awful about her missing her meal because of him.

As he lay on the bed the chest pain grew more acute.

Miraculously my niece Rebecca, who was on our team that week, had decided to drop in to her grandparents' chalet to make arrangements to have lunch with them that day. She was shocked to see Dad lying in agony on the bed and suggested she should go and find a doctor, to which he readily agreed.

Rebecca ran to the Spring Harvest headquarters and they immediately got in touch with the Butlin's medics. She then ran back and told Irene and myself who were with the rest of our team at the Glorie venue.

Although I had no idea what was the matter with him, the news that there was something wrong with Dad again hit me like a bombshell. As Irene and I set off towards my parents' chalet, our team got straight down to prayer. I may be getting on a bit, but it's amazing the speed forty-one-year-old legs can attain when faced with an emergency.

On reaching the chalet Irene and I went in. The medics had just arrived. Whilst I stopped with Dad, Irene left to try and find Mum in the restaurant. As I now looked at Dad, I saw him in a way that I had never seen him before. His face was not covered in blood as it had been when I saw him lying on the concrete in the garden, but now it seemed even worse. I knew this was very serious. His rosy cheeks and healthy complexion had gone. His face was grey.

Mum arrived and, although looking shaken, she seemed very controlled and quite unemotional, which has sometimes been a strength but more often a weakness in our family. It's not that we don't feel emotion—it's just that we have always felt it's a weakness to allow our emotions to show. We laugh a lot together, but I don't think that any of us had ever seen each other cry.

After helping Mum give details about Dad to the nurse, I went outside, feeling awful. Was this the big one? Was this the heart attack that was going to take my father away from me?

It was then that a couple of the Spring Harvest leaders arrived on the scene and, without asking any sort of permission, they grabbed hold of us and started praying for Dad. I have to say that this act of love and concern really stuck in my memory. This was the caring church family in action.

The ambulance arrived and Dad, with Mum at his side, was taken away to Bangor Hospital. I followed soon afterwards in my car. As I sped towards Bangor my mind was in confusion. Should I have stayed and spent time with the children? They were going to wonder where Ishmael was. Should that have been my priority, to carry on with my ministry regardless, and God would honour that and look after Dad?

But then suppose that Dad dies whilst I am with the children? I would never see him again on earth. And what about Mum? She needs me. My mind swung from one way of thinking to the other for the whole of the journey—which on reflection actually helped the time to pass more quickly.

As I arrived at the hospital I met Mum, and the doctor confirmed that Dad was suffering from a severe heart attack and that the next forty-eight hours were critical. We continued to pray, not asking God questions or waiting for answers, just pleading that God would let Dad live.

After looking in on him and seeing that he looked about the same—except for being wired up to a machine in the coronary intensive care unit—I felt it was my responsibility to find Mum some accommodation near the hospital. Whilst she stayed with Dad, I drove round a few local bed and breakfast hostels until I found quite a nice one, but quite a distance away.

When I returned to the hospital I discovered that I needn't have bothered doing this, because the Lord had already sorted out Mum's accommodation. The hospital had kindly agreed to put her up in the nurses' quarters.

We phoned Tim and Heather back in Sussex,

telling them what had happened and they too, fearing the worst, drove up to be with Dad. It was a case of waiting and continued prayer.

It's strange when the expression 'only prayer can save them' is used about anybody, as the Bible says 'the fervent prayer of a righteous man' is more powerful and effective than anything else in the world. Although I knew this scripture, and knew I was fervent enough, I was a little unsure as to whether I was righteous enough.

I remember personally pleading with the Lord to let Dad live—not for ever, but just for a little while longer. I realise that these prayers were selfish and that should Dad die he would be in a much better place in the presence of Jesus, but I still did not want him to go and be with Jesus . . . yet.

From that time until the end of Spring Harvest I felt as if I was in two places at once. I was trying to give my all to the Glorie Company, leading the worship and ministering, whilst my mind was miles away down the road at the hospital.

The forty-eight hours passed and Dad was still alive.

Our thanks went to God. He had answered our prayers once again. We also thanked Him for the way He empowered the medical profession—yes, we praised God for them as well. It was as if Dad had been pulled back to life from the jaws of death. God had been good to us.

Patience and Patient

D ad stayed in Bangor Hospital for about three weeks and then to our great delight returned home.

The doctors had been very helpful before they allowed him to leave. As well as chatting over his condition and convalescence, they also gave him a little book full of strict instructions about what every cardiac victim could do, and more to the point what they should *not* do, to aid recovery. It made my 'no ladder' mandate a couple of years before seem quite tame!

When he arrived home he was understandably very tired and willing to submit to all the doctor's recommendations, which included such devastating demands as no digging in his garden as previously, and quite a long while out of the driver's seat of his car.

But even then, knowing his ever-optimistic character, I knew that as his body regained strength I might need to remind him to live just as the doctor ordered.

And I was right.

As expected, for the first few weeks he was as good as gold and the perfect patient—thankful to be alive and obeying all the instructions to the letter. It helped at this stage that his body kept reminding him of his capabilities, as he soon grew tired and had major problems walking up any hills.

But as his strength continued to return, I saw he was itching to get behind his steering wheel and drive his caravan to pastures new. I was thrilled to see him improving so quickly and did not want to quell his enthusiasm for life, but I was not going to let him drive the car until the doctor's recommended time had expired.

First of all he tried to convince me that if he didn't get back into the driving seat now, he might never get back in it again. That was like water off a duck's back to me. I knew he was a very good driver and there was no way that after over forty years of driving, a few months off the road were going to make him lose his confidence. He's obviously forgotten that he's brought me up to think like him, and his plea sounded very similar to a tactic that I would use to try and get my own way.

He didn't stop there though—he went to a higher authority. He managed to find a local doctor who thought the same way he did.

But again I put a firm foot down, saying that as it was the Bangor doctors who knew more about his condition than anyone, we would stick with their advice. He reluctantly had to agree.

It's sometimes very hard for parents to obey their children.

I've hinted before at one of Dad's failings, which was highlighted during those few months without the use of his wheels. Although he knew that one of the Church's functions was mutual support in times of need, Dad loved putting himself out for others but had trouble allowing people to put themselves out for him. Many would offer to drive him here, there and everywhere, but although he genuinely appreciated their offers, he always felt he was being an inconvenience to them.

I suppose it was made even worse for him when he could stand and stare at a redundant car stuck in his drive, with his mind assuring him that he was now fit and able to drive. I'd never thought about it until now, but it seems a shame that Mum never learned to drive. Maybe both partners should take up the challenge of a driving test, because you never know, at some stage, even later on in life, it could make a whole lot of difference.

But Dad's grounding soon passed and his patience paid off. He proved his previous conjecture wrong by still managing to be able to drive, which came as no surprise to me. And the reward for his patience and for being a good boy was to be told that his heart was now much stronger than it had been before the attack.

He was thrilled to be mobile again—not just on

two legs but on four wheels. I was still not happy with him driving the car with a heavy caravan in tow, but as there was nothing in the heart attack recoverers' rule book to say that he shouldn't, I could find no reason to try to say a dogmatic 'no'.

Dad was, however, noticeably more cautious with his lifestyle, because he knew that not just my eyes, but those of all the members of our family, would be watching him to make sure that he wasn't going to overdo things again. This was not just for his sake. None of us wanted to have to go through the North Wales experience with him again.

We were all thrilled to see Dad back to his old self. Life was once more filled with church, holidays, joking, laughing, eating and drinking—only the last two were curtailed due to a diet the doctor had put him on.

It felt great having Dad back as I was now ministering not just in Europe but in America. Again he would sit in front of the television with great interest as I showed him one hall after the next, one audience after the other. I'm sure each venue must have looked like the last one and he must have found them rather tedious, but he never let on about it. I was so grateful to God for giving him this new lease of life.

As I mentioned, a year and a half passed between the ladder accident and the North Wales heart attack. Strangely enough it was exactly a year and a half before the next painful problem arose.

Although, as I said, Dad was a humble man, he still found certain things embarrassing. Now he was having trouble passing water and was told that he had prostate trouble. We thought nothing much of it as most men have this sort of trouble later on in life and medical science has many ways of dealing with this reasonably minor problem.

Dad found it quite humiliating living with a catheter inserted in him, but during the wait for a hospital bed it was the only answer to get rid of the urine. For two months he shuffled around the house in this condition. To begin with he tried to act as if it wasn't there, and even managed to drive his car, but as time went on, he found that this was a luxury that he would have to give up as it was proving to be much too painful.

We British are a nation who are used to waiting for everything. We wait at bus stops, train stations, post offices, shops, courtrooms, airports, and so the list could go on. I do think it's bad news though, that people in pain have to wait for treatment. Having to wait months, sometimes years, for a hospital bed seems wrong. I appreciate that Dad's troubles were not an emergency or life-threatening, and quite rightly the serious infirmities should always be given priority; but it does not seem right that anyone should have to suffer for ages when cures are waiting, ready and available in a big building down the road. Eventually Dad was admitted to the local hospital and had an operation. We were all relieved for Dad's sake that it was now all over and he could get back to normal.

But there was no change afterwards.

Then another operation followed.

Still no change.

Although we had never stopped praying and hoping for a healing of the water problem, we were beginning to be concerned. If a prostate operation is such a simple one, why is it that Dad had been in pain for three months and each operation had failed?

It was Christmas Eve when Mum and I confronted the doctor to ask what was really wrong. She hesitated and explained that she couldn't tell us before she told Dad, so we asked if she could tell him now whilst we were there, then we could all hear what she had to say together. She agreed.

The doctor told us the worst—and we then understood why she had hesitated. It was cancer. A malignant tumour in the prostate. We were told that nothing could be done to get rid of it but that monthly injections might slow down its growth.

The very word 'cancer' cannot be whispered. It's a word that shrieks out at you, and the word 'malignant' emphasises it all the more. I wrestled with this word in prayer for quite a while and found that it is in fact more destructive than the disease. It's a word that can easily rock your faith and if it's allowed to, it can put question marks over the whole area of divine healing.

In our church we were very fortunate because one of our young Mums had been miraculously healed of breast cancer. So it did not mean the beginning of the end in my mind—it just meant the beginning of a lot more fervent prayer.

This being the case, I would not allow my mind to consider that this was anywhere near the end of Dad. After all there was no blood on his face and he wasn't a frightening shade of grey. I'd seen him look a lot worse over the past couple of years, so I was very optimistic that the Lord was going to bring him through this.

Even when my faith level dipped a bit, I knew there were still the monthly injections. They might be God's answer. I could even imagine the doctors' faces when they saw that the impossible had happened and the injections had not only restricted new cancer growth but also shrivelled up the old one.

It was on 27 December that Dad was brought home, still well attached to his catheter, which had become a vital part of him for the last four months.

Again the church and family rejoiced in the fact that Dad was back, and he certainly looked good. There was a lot of life in him yet.

Mind you, there were some changes. Dad was always one who would make the most of every opportunity to talk about Jesus to those who did not know Him, but now there seemed to be a new sort of urgency. He didn't wait for opportunities—he made them. He lived as though he had no idea how much longer he was going to be around, so he was going to make the most of every minute he was here.

It was while he was taking his mind off his own temporary problems, and keeping it upon eternal problems concerning others, that he had his best experience for a long time. At the end of January his catheter was taken out and he was able to pass water normally.

I must confess I rarely praise God for such mundane things as normal bodily functions—I just take them for granted. I guess it's not until they stop working normally that we realise how important they are. So to end this chapter—after five months of discomfort Dad received a wonderful belated Christmas present from the Lord. I can still hear him breathe that wonderful sigh of relief as he thanked the Lord.

Wonders and Signs

With the catheter gone and now just an uncomfortable part of Dad's memories, his holiday programme was back on the agenda and totally extreme even by his standards. It was as though something (or someone) told him that he didn't have long, so he was going allout to make sure that he and Mum were going to enjoy to the full whatever time they might have left together.

In a matter of months he had holidayed in the Isle of Wight, Swanage, Sidmouth, Cullompton and the New Forest. As you may have gathered, he was very partial to the West Country. The two wheels on his little old pride and joy, the caravan, must have been red hot.

Towards the end of the summer when he and Mum went to the New Forest, my daughter Suzy and I thought we would give them a surprise by dropping in to see them.

We managed to struggle up at the crack of dawn and arrived by breakfast time at their caravan site, where the sun was shining full strength on a few righteous . . . and probably many more unrighteous. But the sun was not our problem. The difficulty we now faced was that the site was big and full of trees, gorse bushes, ponies, and believe it or not, caravans. The latter were every shape and size imaginable— some extremely flash, and others that would have looked more at home parked on the side of a motor- way for the road-repairers to sit and sup their coffees in! How were amateur non-campers such as Suzy and I supposed to track them down?

We drove very slowly right around the perimeter road and it was quite embarrassing. People in the middle of performing all sorts of domestic functions stood staring indignantly at us. It was as if we had deliberately invaded their space and took pleasure in spying on them. Strange folk these one-week-a-year woodland dwellers!

After completing the full circle, we reached the entrance where we first started. It was then that we caught a glimpse of Dad. He was, as expected, as brown as the proverbial berry and walking back from the site shop with his beloved breakfast ready to throw into the frying pan. That was another thing about Dad. If you wanted to go on holiday and be sure that the sun was going to shine, forget about the weatherman's rather hit-and-miss predictions. You'd do better just to follow that caravan when it pulled out of my parents' drive.

His face beamed when he saw us. He was thrilled that we had called down to see him. I couldn't get over how well and healthy he looked. Whilst Suzy and

I were sitting outside his caravan frying in the hot sunshine, Mum was inside frying the sausages. Dad just seemed to be getting in the way trying to help.

I can't remember ever seeing him so relaxed, happy and contented. As we drove away, looking back at the radiant couple waving and full of excitement, who could have guessed that this was going to be the last time that Dad would ever camp in the New Forest or enjoy a holiday in his little old caravan.

The elders of our church, who included me in their number, were thrilled with Dad's progress. Due to his ill health we had relieved him of any official duties, but now, as he seemed so much better, we thought it was time he was given a further dose of responsibility.

It must have been strange for the 'Patriarch Apostle', 'Founder Elder', or whatever title you care to put upon him, now to be offered the role of a house group leader. Some I dare say may have felt insulted or offended if put in a similar position, allowing pride and self-pity to creep in and convince them they had been demoted.

Not Dad. He never worried about titles or positions. He just wanted to stay in a place where he could continue to be used by God. He happily agreed to take on the new task. He even suggested that if we ever thought of planting out another congregation in the near future we should not rule him out as being part of it.

Although Dad looked and acted healthy during these months, and he continued to receive his monthly injection, a pain in his back was getting steadily worse.

He never seemed to grumble much about it. All he would say is, 'I wonder what the Lord is trying to show me now?' and that would lead us all into a long discussion and debate. But with all the talking we never really fathomed out an answer.

The doctor of course had more professional and non-debatable ideas about the backache. His qualified opinion told us that the injections were not doing any good and the cancer was starting to spread. When we asked the specialist what would happen next, all he would say was, 'Come and see me again when something happens.'

I found this sort of comment quite aggravating. I could see that Dad was in a lot of pain and the painkillers seemed to be of little use, yet we were just told to watch out for something—but we hadn't a clue as to what we were supposed to be watching out for!

I was now going round each morning to see him, and as I entered the door Mum would whisper to me a one-line update. One day she would whisper, 'He's rather low,' another day 'He hasn't slept all night.' But every day, as soon as I walked into the front room and saw Dad sitting in his usual chair, he always had a smile and was ever so pleased to see me.

Each day my first question was to ask him how he felt and his answer was always the same. He would say he was in a lot of pain. But instead of elaborating on his condition, he would then go on to say that that was enough about him and ask me what I had been up to.

Throughout this period my parents were really being blessed by a book called *Diamonds in the Dust* written by a very brave woman of God called Joni Eareckson. The book contained daily readings and comments, and what made them so encouraging to Mum and Dad was that Joni herself had been confined to a wheelchair for many years. So when she spoke on disability and suffering she knew exactly what she was talking about. Most days they would share with me Joni's 'thought for the day' as they believed that certain things she had written were very relevant to Dad's situation.

Dad was also encouraged by my videos and exciting stories about people becoming Christians in every place I played. Some days he was more excited than I was. On days when Dad felt worse I found it hard to be enthusiastic about anything, as I looked at him and thought of the agony he was suffering.

Another sign that things were not improving was that Dad's wrist was giving him constant pain, which in turn now started to restrict his writing. Many years before after I had written my autobiography *The History of Ishmael*, I realised that Dad had a wealth of interesting stories that would be both encouraging to the Christian and a challenge to those who were not yet Christians. I encouraged him to start writing it all down, which he had been doing. This wrist difficulty meant that every word he wrote was going to be a painful experience. But needless to say he kept on writing.

In the late autumn he went on what was to be his last holiday. He didn't take the caravan, but went and stayed with some very close friends in a lovely house near Dartmouth in Devon. Although he loved it down there and was able to read, write, sleep and sit in front of a roaring log fire, I know he didn't go down for any selfish reasons.

I wonder now if he had any idea that this was likely to be the last time that he and Mum were going to be able to have a holiday together. I also wonder if he knew that it might be the last time that he would see his close friends, and the main reason that he went was that he wanted to let them see that even in all his pain he would never stop praising Jesus.

On returning home I noticed that Dad was finding it very difficult to bend or stand. He explained to the doctor that he had a lot of pain on his right side slightly below the waist and right across the back. He was given another scan and then the doctor told us that the problem had now entered the bones.

Health and Healing

I now knew that Dad was seriously ill, but I could not see that this illness was going to kill him. I still believed that what the doctors couldn't deal with, the Lord would.

I realise that it's getting to the point where I am becoming very emotional about what I am writing. So I want to pull back from Dad for a while, become more general, and then tell you about two small friends of mine.

It's worth pointing out at this stage how the main emphasis of my ministry does change approximately every two years. I'm sure the Lord leads me to this so that I don't become complacent and rely upon my own expertise and strength. This way it seems that just when I am becoming reasonably confident in one area, the Lord moves me on to another, so all the time I have to cry out to Him for help.

A few years ago I majored on deliverance, then after that healing, then prophecy, and for the last couple of years it really has been just straightforward salvation. Of course that didn't mean that I packed up praying for the sick or prophesying. All it meant was that it took a much lower profile, especially in the all-age celebrations that I travelled around doing each week.

Personally, as I have prayed for people, I have discovered a few reasons why some are not healed—some biblical, some common sense, and others both biblical and common sense! I write these down, not so that you give up praying for the sick, but so that you realise that if somebody isn't instantly healed, it might not be your lack of faith that is stopping the healing taking place.

Allow me to give you just a few of them:

1. Unbelief (Matthew 13) If Jesus could do hardly any healings because of the people's unbelief, what hope will we have with certain people?

2. Some don't mind living with their illness because that's what gets people talking to them and gives them attention. We won't be able to ask God to release them of some illness that they want to hang on to for whatever reason.

3. An ailment can keep people humble. For example, I don't think that Jacob's hip joint would have been healed however much prayer it had been given, or even Paul's thorn in the flesh (assuming that was not referring to his wife).

4. Disobedience (Acts 11:29–30) If someone is messed up at the communion table, it is senseless to pray for them until they have sorted things out with Jesus.

5. (John 5:14) Stop sinning or something worse may happen to you, and that means worse than

being paralysed. As with all sin, deliberate sin needs to be confessed before forgiveness (and healing) can take place.

6. Stupid things we inflict on our own bodies. Who's going to bother to pray for a smoker's cough, a glutton's stomach problem or a drunkard's hangover or liver complaint? It also seems just as silly to me to pray for weight problems (when a person refuses to exercise), restless nights (when a person is deliberately overworking) and certain stresses and fears that have come about by watching rubbish on television. The prayer of faith will do little until other more important areas are put right by the sufferer.

7. Testing of our faith (James 1:2). It's easy to praise God when we are one hundred per cent healthy. I have no trouble believing that the Lord allows us to have some 'sickness' trials for a season to see if we still praise when we are a bit under the weather. Again, if the Lord is allowing a person to suffer these trials, they will be conquered as the individual praises God in them, not by means of the prayer of faith bringing him or her out of them—Job being a classic example.

8. Punishment. Any volunteers to pray for Ananias and Sapphira's heart problems, King Herod's worm problem, Nebuchadnezzar's hair and eating disorder, Elymas' and the men of Sodom's sight difficulties, Gehazi's leprosy? . . . and so the list goes on. I think you have got the point.

9. A sign from God (Luke 1). I dare anyone to pray for Zechariah before he wrote down 'His name is John'!

10. Finally, and I guess most important, is divine sovereignty. I know we may always say these words when we don't know the answer to something —but so we must. God doesn't live by our rules and demands. He is the only one Who knows what is perfect, right and just. As He is the one Who actually does all the healing anyway, I'm sure He has a time for a person to be healed, and that may not always be the same time that is in our mind. He also has a perfect time for a person to be born and, maybe the hardest thing for us humans to understand, a perfect time for a person to die.

Why is this hard to understand? Please read the following letters about the two small friends of mine that I mentioned earlier.

My first little friend was a ten-year-old boy called Matthew who had always suffered with a kidney disorder. His parents kindly sent me the following, which is part of a special leaflet that was printed for his funeral.

As a child growing up in our home, Matthew had always been mischievous with a glint in his big blue eyes. At Easter, we went as a family to a Christian conference called Spring Harvest. Matthew was in a children's group called 'the Glorie Company'. During that week Matthew came to know and love the Lord Jesus in a special way and we saw the change in him.

Just before Christmas Matthew went on a kidney transplant list. After a lovely time at Christmas, Matthew's favourite time of the year, on 30 December we had our call. Matthew was so excited about this. In his words, 'This is my best Christmas present.' He enjoyed his time on Dickens Ward and staying at the Macdonald House, especially playing with the Nintendo. He recovered well initially, but then after three and a half weeks at home, he was admitted for the final time. All the time he fought bravely, but in the end there was too big a mountain to climb. Matthew went to be with his Lord on 31 May.

We know that Matthew will be greatly missed by us and many of you, but we have a sure hope that where Matthew has gone, is far, far better than here; and one day we will be with him again.

When asked in hospital, 'How are you today Matthew?' he would reply, 'Much better' whether he really was or not. Now he can really say he's much better. Matthew's red hat that so many of you associate with him had a badge on it saying 'I am a Glorie'. Well now he is, praise God.

My second little friend was a seven-year-old called Philip. Here is an extract from the letter that his parents kindly sent me.

Dear Ishmael, you were very special to Philip. Philip started enjoying your music when he was two or three.

On Sunday 14 April Philip, then aged four, had tonsillitis and was unable to go to Sunday school. His Dad stayed at home with him whilst his Mum went to church with his brother Ian. A few weeks before, the morning service from Arun Christian Fellowship had been broadcast, which we had videoed. Philip sat with his Dad and watched this, obviously enjoying the music. You talked for a while about becoming a Christian. Towards the end Philip suddenly turned to his Dad and said 'I want to become a Christian.' Initially flabbergasted, Dad recovered and they said a prayer of commitment together.

Since then Philip has been a typical boy, but talked to Jesus every day and several times said 'I love Jesus more than anyone else.' Ishmael, thank you for your music.

We found that the spiritual depth of some of your songs sparked off a number of deep conversations with Philip when he asked questions about the Holy Spirit, Satan and angels, to name but a few.

One morning Philip went to school feeling perfectly healthy, but at 3.10 when we arrived to pick him up we were told that Philip was not well. Immediately phone calls were made and at least twenty people started praying.

At 2.40 Philip had had a headache and then been sick in the playground. Later he was sick again and, feeling faint, was kept inside till we arrived. By the time we arrived he had almost lost consciousness, but signified that he knew we had arrived. We took him to casualty but he never regained consciousness. They had diagnosed a brain haemorrhage and sadly he died in the theatre at around 11 p.m.

The funeral was on 31 March. Three hundred packed the church. It contained many of your songs. *Father God I Wonder*—many people love this and Philip knew the words from a very early age—*Little Lamb*, followed by *Little Soldier*.

The committal service at the crematorium started with *Angels* and finished while the coffin was going away with your instrumental *Mission Accomplished*. This was absolutely right. Philip's mission on earth was over. The music from *Mission Accomplished* is so triumphant without being trite, but I don't think we will ever listen to it again without crying tears of sadness and joy.

My love goes out to Andy, Denise, David, Peter, Laura and Stephen; also to Mike, Kath and Ian. Thanks.

Why did these two young saints die? I haven't got a clue. They may have seen an answer in one of the songs that they loved singing.

Praise God that both the families are managing to live with the grief, and I guess many unanswered questions, but still believing that God's timing is perfect. Far from knocking their faith, it has in fact deepened their faith in God.

I studied again some of the lyrics from the songs that I had written, that Matthew and Philip loved.

LITTLE LAMB

Little lamb please heed my warning,
Beware the night is coming fast.
But little lamb don't fear the darkness,
The shepherd's light won't let it last.
He will keep you, love you, hold you,
But don't you stray from His embrace.
Greater love has not been known,
The shepherd died in the lamb's place.

LITTLE SOLDIER

Little soldier you are facing
A hard life ahead,
The road is still rough and steep.
When you're faint and you're weary
The Bible has said
Father won't leave you alone,
Leave you alone—no not leave you alone,
Father won't leave you alone.
The age draws to an end as Jesus your friend
Is preparing for you to come home.

ANGELS

What a long hard day it's been,
To take His cross will mean you'll suffer pain.
Though you're weak He'll keep you clean,
Rest in Him and be renewed again.
But forget the wars you've been in today
As nothing can disturb you now
'Cause round your bed are stationed heaven's armies.
Just lay down weary child lay down,
Little angel go to sleep
'Cause Father's here and He will keep you safe,
'Cause Father's here and He will keep you safe.

They are safe now.

Although it broke my heart reading these letters, I was thrilled that my songs were blessing and helping others in differing circumstances because that was the reason I had written them. But as yet I had never had to apply them to my experiences in life.

Dad was still alive, and although I hadn't heard anything from the Lord I was fairly sure that he was going to pull through. After all, I was pretty sure that there was still uncompleted work that he needed to finish.

Fame and Fortune

It had been an incredibly busy autumn for me. As well as the tours to the States, I had also had a lot of ministry opportunities throughout Britain. The little spare time that I had was more than occupied with recording a new album, plus the ongoing elder's work in the local church.

Important as all these were, I made it a priority to spend as much time as humanly possible with Dad. He was now in great pain with his back, and whilst we still prayed with all our might for his healing, our prayers were not being answered. We couldn't even seem to get the Lord to release him from the pain. This was confusing. Why didn't God respond to our prayers?

In mid-December two memorable things stand out in my mind. The first was a very happy occasion when we had our annual elders' and wives' Christmas meal together.

It was my job to find and reserve ten seats at a restaurant, which is not as easy to accomplish as it sounds. I mean, it's reasonably easy for elders to agree on worship, teaching etc., but once you get discussing food, there seems to be more debate and contradicting ideas than there would be discussing the five points of Calvinism!

Christmas approached rapidly, and as always we found a compromise date and a restaurant, and I paid the deposits. A few days later a leader and his wife had to cancel, because he was working somewhere in Korea that day.

Well, disappointment was turned to joy for Dad and Mum as, with no hesitation and very little notice, they were happy to occupy the two vacant seats.

This is where you could see Dad at his best. His post-heart-attack diet was now not quite so strictly adhered to, and he was guaranteed to be the life and soul of the party. He was great fun to be with.

There is no way anyone on any of the surrounding tables that evening would have guessed that the person who was bringing so much entertainment to all the others around him, was very seriously ill and in a lot of pain.

The second thing that stands out in my mind was that the BBC had been in touch with me to ask if they could film a programme called *This is the Day*, live from my house on Sunday 2 January.

I love working on television. It's such a great medium to put across the wonderful message of the Lord Jesus to millions of people who do not yet know Him.

After agreeing to do it, long discussions took place with the producer over the content of the show and which people should be invited into my lounge that morning to take part. The idea was to treat it like a normal Sunday, when our house is always busy with various friends rushing in and out.

We decided that as well as my immediate family—Irene, Joseph, Daniel and Suzy—it would be good to invite certain of my friends, making sure that we had a good cross-section of ages.

We had to make sure that we had a little baby, a host of teenagers, some married couples in their twenties, and an older couple. I must admit that although my father and mother were my first choice for the older couple, I had a slight reservation about Dad, which was nothing to do with his illness.

A few years earlier I had been part of another live television broadcast. The Independent Television Network had come to film our church at worship on a Sunday morning. This was Dad's first and only other television appearance.

In case you readers don't understand, live television means just that. What happens on that morning is what the viewers will see in their homes—there is no chance to edit anything.

Anyway, on this particular occasion, Dad was asked to say a prayer. During the rehearsals Dad prayed, but I felt his prayer was far too short and he was obviously nervous. I encouraged him to relax and not to think about the cameras and the millions of viewers. I told him to do what he would normally do, and just think about the Lord.

Well, all I can say was that he certainly did; and I'm sure any of you who watched that programme will remember me discreetly trying to pull the microphone away from him as he got so involved in his prayer. I was frightened that after he had finished, there would only be time left for the closing credits.

We had a great laugh with Dad about this every time we mentioned the programme thereafter, and after watching it, he too could see the funny side.

So here was my predicament. Another programme, another viewing audience of millions, yet the same father.

It was decided that rather than have Dad pray, where he might close his eyes and miss us all frantically waving at him if he went on too long again, we should ask him just to say a few words. This seemed much safer.

As the month of December continued, so his pain increased. On 19 December I woke up early and went for a walk along the beach to pray about Dad's cancer. The next day he was going back into hospital and I still had no idea of God's plan. It was then, as I walked along on that cold winter's morning, that I felt I had my first word from the Lord, and that was to read Hebrews 11:1. The verse reads, 'Now faith is being sure of what we hope for and certain of what we do not see.'

I had read this verse many times before, but somehow it now took on a new relevance.

My hope was that the cancer and pain would leave Dad's body, but just how sure was I that this was going to happen, or more to the point, how sure was I that this was what God wanted to happen?

I just had to keep repeating, 'Lord help my unbelief', because every time I allowed my mind to think of Dad, I couldn't be certain of what I could not see. All I could be certain of was that he was in a lot of pain.

Early the following morning I went round and read Hebrews 11:1 to Dad and shared my thoughts with him. Although I guess none of us were still totally convinced of what God was doing, this was the first word of any sort, let alone encouragement. So we decided as a family that we were going to hang on to this scripture against all odds, and try to remain sure of what we all hoped for.

Later that day Dad did return to hospital and was given an X-ray, then a double dose of radiotherapy to the second and third vertebrae in his spine. He was told that he would have immense pain for a few days, then the pain should calm down. I really felt that this was to be the beginning of an improvement. At last Dad was on the mend.

In fact it seemed to work the opposite way. For the first twenty-four hours the pain left off for a time, but for the next ten days he was confined to his bed as he couldn't even bend his body. He was then given much stronger painkillers.

All the family got together to try and make Dad's bedroom a more enjoyable world to live in. He had now moved out of his own bedroom with Mum and for reasons of comfort was now in a single bed in the spare room. We fitted up the television and video in a position where he wouldn't have to move to watch it. We made sure everything of importance was as accessible as it could be and we lined up many visitors, not so much to break up the long hours, but more to try and take his mind off the pain.

Christmas celebrations were not the same. It was as if there was a massive gap in the congregation of the usually exuberant Christmas morning family service, and that gap was confined to lying in bed wishing he had been well enough to be with us.

But then came a strange turn in events.

We were only a few days away from the television broadcast, and Dad was still unable to leave his bed, let alone spend many hours around my house for rehearsals.

I had still made no alternative plans, as I was convinced that somehow the Lord was going to make him well enough to be there. The programme was due to be filmed on the Sunday and it was on the Thursday prior to it that Dad suddenly started to feel better. He was able to get up and very cautiously move around.

On the Saturday we had to rehearse from 12.30 to 6.00 p.m. and except for a thirty-minute lie down, Dad miraculously managed to stay smiling, whilst propped up in a chair for the whole time.

I remember how exhausted he looked as he left for home that evening, and I prayed that he would be refilled with supernatural strength and energy to cope with the following morning.

Early on the Sunday morning the thirty film crew returned. They joined the three articulated outside broadcast lorries that were making quite a successful job of blocking my road. Also a crane had parked in next door's garden, and what looked like a satellite dish was looking down at us from one hundred feet up in the sky.

All this fascinated Dad when he arrived and out came his camera to record the event for posterity. He then entered the house and took his place in his chair, still quite unsure as to what he was going to say.

It was then I suggested that maybe it would be good to mention his cancer, as a lot of the viewers might be suffering similar trouble themselves, or know of loved ones in that position.

The programme ran wonderfully well, with no problems, but on reflection Dad's few words seemed to be one of the most effective things that happened on it.

Numbers of people have since come up and told me how touched they were by what he said, and they only knew the half of what he was going through at the time. Hopefully this book will give you insight into the other half.

During the programme I told the story of the wise and foolish men and how both felt the storm and rain, but the man who had built his life on the rock (the Lord Jesus) didn't collapse when the pressure was on. Dad followed it by saying the following: 'We're talking about storms in our life. Well, Dorothy and I are going through a storm at present. I have been diagnosed as having cancer. But it's how we trust in these situations when all these storms come about. Also we would like to say how wonderful it is to have the encouragement of people and their prayers at this time.'

Hardly mind-blowing oratory, but when coming from a very sick man whose face and conviction shone out louder than his words, it made the hardest cynic sit up and listen.

Doctors and Nurses

After the television programme Irene and I went away for a few days, as the preparation and filming, plus the previous chaotic year, were beginning to take their toll. I always try to keep a few days free at the start of a new year to clear my head of the last twelve months and receive a new enthusiasm and a fresh vision from God for the year to come.

We didn't travel far, so thanks to the telephone I was able to keep in touch with Dad's progress, and if there were any dramatic changes I could easily be back within a couple of hours. Although we had a good time, it was as if there was a dark cloud of uncertainty hanging over our heads.

Dad was as well as could be expected—having given his all over the filming period—and was now totally exhausted and spent the next few days back in his bed. Whilst lying there he decided to put one of his most quoted verses of the Bible into action. 'Is any one of you sick? He should call the elders of the church to pray over him and anoint him with oil in the name of the Lord. And the prayer offered in faith will make the sick person well; the Lord will raise him up. If he has sinned he will be forgiven' (James 5:14–15).

This had always been one of Dad's favourite Bible verses which he had used successfully many times in the past, and I'm sure as the elders came around and prayed for him and anointed him with oil, he had no reason to believe that it wouldn't be successful again. After the prayer he felt better in himself, but there was no obvious improvement to his body.

As the monthly injections continued, so the pain still seemed to be increasing. By the end of the first week of January, Dad found that although he was able to spend quite a few hours of the day sitting in a chair, it was getting too painful to walk far.

I've already mentioned that Dad was a keen gardener, and I believe that I have also mentioned that I was not. In my massive garden only two things seemed to grow with intense vigour and without any encouragement or help from me, come drought or flood—grass and weeds!

As a sort of half-joke in the TV programme when asked about any New Year resolutions, I couldn't think of an answer, so gazing through the window at my horticultural nightmare, I said that I might spend more time gardening.

I deliberately didn't look at Dad when I said it, because I feared he might have taken me seriously and started handing on his boring old gardening magazines to me when he had finished reading them.

On 14 January—on what proved to be his last visit to my house—for some strange reason I asked Dad to plan out my garden for me so it would be easier for me to keep tidy.

I could see that my request had not only taken him by surprise, but it had also given him a lot of pleasure.

He left our lounge, just about managed to walk down to the end of the garden, and with some paper and a pencil did a quick drawing, gave it to me and then started painfully to retrace his steps.

Whilst he was making his way slowly across my huge expanse of grass, which at some time had been a lawn, I reminded him of a lean-to shed that he had nearly finished making for me, which would give my mower a new home and leave more room in my garage for all my Glorie products, musical equipment and so on. I told him to hurry up and get well again so that he could come and finish it off.

He chuckled as he told me not to worry, he hadn't forgotten. It was as though he expected to come back in a few days and complete it.

Immediately I started work on my garden following Dad's plan to the letter. Why was I doing it? Had I suddenly inherited green fingers or was I doing it so Dad would be proud of me? I honestly didn't know. However, within a few days of blood, sweat, and tears (including successfully whacking my guitar-playing finger with a club hammer which turned the nail a dark blue), my garden looked great. I only wish that Dad had been able to come round at least one more time just to be able to see it.

Dad's biggest worry was not the pain, it was the thought of being a burden on Mum. He hated not being able to do the usual tasks that he had always done around the house to help her out, and I believe at times he felt useless. In his diary he wrote these words:

> I had a good cry to the Lord many times—He is my Father and loves me but I have to tell Him truthfully I cannot bear any more pain, and call upon Him to help me and Dorothy. I trust my God. I don't understand many things, but I just want my life to glorify Him. I seek to rejoice in the situation I am in—but I couldn't without His help and His peace in me. I particularly pray for Dorothy who sees me in so much pain and disablement and cannot do anything about it.

During this time no one seemed to be able to find any drug that could relieve the pain, and it was then that someone mentioned that a hospice might be able to help.

Dad's first reaction to that word was far from favourable. In fact I remember him saying that in his experience a hospice is a place where people go to die.

I must admit that until this point I had no idea what a hospice was. I thought that it was just a little private hospital where the rich could go to avoid being with the lower classes of society.

With no other alternatives left we unanimously felt it was certainly worth investigating.

Dad got the ball rolling by mentioning it to his consultant, who in turn told him to contact his local doctor, who would in turn contact the local hospice for us. The one we decided to ask for help was called St Barnabas', which was situated just a few miles down the road. We rang our local doctor who assured us he would get in touch with St Barnabas'.

Then came all sorts of encouraging comments. We heard (second-hand of course) that these hospice people were geniuses. They knew all about cancer; they knew what sort of painkillers to use; they knew all about their patients. In fact it looked as if they were the answer to all our prayers and Dad's problems.

Day after day whilst Dad was in agony, we waited for the phone to ring, but nothing happened. We were told that they would contact us immediately, but immediately was now nine days later.

With no help a further complication had set in and yet another embarrassing one—bowel problems resulting in severe constipation. After four days of not being able to pass a motion, a doctor came and gave him some medicine that did nothing. After six days a Christian friend of ours, who also happened to be a nurse, contacted St Barnabas' to find out why they had not been in contact with Dad.

The surprised and apologetic St Barnabas' had to confess they had never heard of Dad. It seems our local doctor had forgotten to contact them.

This is one of those times when it is easy to get

angry, especially as a lot of Dad's suffering could have been dealt with days before if it hadn't been for what looked like incompetence.

We discussed it as a family and my mother convinced me that we could not blame people, because we were still very confident that Dad was in the Lord's hands, not the doctor's. Maybe we were putting just a little bit too much hope in what man could do.

Anyway, by the time our nursing friend had made a few phone calls, not only had St Barnabas' been informed, but the cavalry had been alerted in the form of a lady doctor who arrived fully armed with a suppository or two, explaining that we only had to ring and she would be back whenever duty called. She did however advise us not to wait so long next time, for both the patient sake and her own. I think we got her point.

On 26 January I was doing some preparation for a talk on deliverance and I thought that the timing of this might have some significance for Dad. I knew that he did not seem to be getting any better, so I thought I would go around and pray for him in case any demons were slowing down his recovery.

I believe that Jesus has given us authority over evil, so in the name of Jesus I cast out anything that came to mind, ranging from the spirit of cancer to the spirit of death. After I had finished praying and Dad thanked me, I honestly felt that no demons could have survived the onslaught of such a purge. Without doubt the power of Jesus would have blasted into oblivion anything inside Dad that should not have been. Yet with all my prayers of deliverance, Dad was still in pain.

On the last day of January, before I went round to spend the morning with Dad, I spoke to another of our local doctors and I have to confess I didn't quite manage to live up to Mum's forgiving attitude towards forgetfulness. Although I made it very clear that I in no way blamed the medical profession for my father's condition, I fear that he may have gone away with a slight hint that I was a little angry with what I thought was negligence shown by his partner.

Later that morning Dad and I met a doctor from St Barnabas'. He was a really nice person who kept cracking jokes. It all started because he had the same surname as a famous brand of beer, which he certainly had a few quips about. I guessed this was a set patter he often used to help put his future patients at ease, and it worked. We were soon all smiling as he continued his repertoire between each sip of coffee. This was the first time I had seen a doctor laughing on duty. I suppose that given all the sad and depressing sights that he saw, being jovial must have helped to keep him alive.

He told us all about the hospice, making it very clear to Dad that it was not just a place like Boot Hill where people go to die. In fact it was the opposite to that. By the time he'd finished talking about it, it sounded so wonderful that I was half expecting Dad to book up next year's holiday there.

There was just one serious point in the conversation which I do recall. He had obviously seen Dad's medical records and knew a lot more about Dad's condition than we did, and he put over very subtly that Dad's long-term future did not look promising.

I wasn't too upset by this comment though. Long-term could be ten to twenty years—and also this guy may not have been a Christian, so it was unlikely that he had been informed about the date that God had chosen for Dad's departure.

9

Fact and Faith

As January passed and the crisp and frosty month of February began, Dad had to go back to the local hospital to be told the result of a scan that he had had previously.

He was still in pain but felt he could make the five-mile journey in his car. But of course he was not able to drive. Mum and I helped Dad carefully into the car as he was now rather fragile, whilst my brother Tim volunteered to be chauffeur and settled himself into the driving seat.

What a horrific journey it proved to be. From the moment we moved out of the drive Dad seemed to be in more pain than I had ever seen him in before. My guess was that it was due to the immense pressure being put on the now crumbling backbone.

It was like *déjà vu*. A few years before—which was where this nightmare began—I was doing the same journey, to the same hospital, with the same man in pain after falling from the ladder; but it wasn't quite history repeating itself, as now Dad was definitely in a lot more pain and since that time he had also suffered the heart attack.

As again we all prayed in tongues, my fear was now

not the cancer, it was whether Dad's heart would be strong enough to cope with the unrelenting agony that he was suffering. Although we were told that his heart was strong, I couldn't help wondering how strong it really was and how much of this trip it could take.

After what seemed like the longest five miles that any of us have ever had to travel, we eventually pulled up outside the hospital. I don't know if you have ever noticed, but when hospitals are built the planners never seem to consider that relatives and friends may wish to visit the poor patients inside. That is why they always seem to have few or no parking facilities.

This being the case here, it was decided that I should leap out and run and find a nurse who would hopefully know the best way to transport Dad (who now looked terrible) from the inside of the car to the inside of the building.

Now I have to say that I know as much about hospitals as I do about hospices, which if you can remember from the last chapter is zero. I rushed through the door in sheer panic looking for anyone who in any way resembled a nurse. It was then that a lady, who because of her uniform looked very much like a nurse, called over to me. 'Excuse me,' she said, 'are you Ishmael?' I was stunned and as I turned to her and told her I was, she told me she had watched the New Year TV programme and how much she had enjoyed it.

I must admit I thought, 'Isn't God brilliant! Here I am rushing around trying to find help and God has made sure the right person is standing right by the door waiting for us.'

Normally at this stage I would very much have liked to have a long chat about the programme, but obviously there were more pressing needs. In no time this wonderful nurse had Dad lying comfortably on a bed and was chatting to him about his part on the show. As Dad lay there allowing the vicious burning pains of the cancer to subside, I could see he too knew that the Lord had prepared the way for us.

After a cup of tea, the four of us waited for the consultant to join us, in a room so small that I was relegated to sitting on the radiator. I'm afraid the consultant was not a barrel of laughs like our doctor from St Barnabas'. Mind you, none of us could even have forced a smile with the news that he shared.

He told us that the cancer had spread and that he was going to book Dad in at another hospital for more radiotherapy. When we asked if this would help, all he could say was that it might. He also arranged for Dad to be measured up for a special corset that might strengthen his backbone and hopefully relieve some of the pain.

Tim and I left Mum and Dad and wandered down the corridor to a desk where we had to pay in advance for the corset; then we made our way to the pharmacy where another Christian friend of ours from the church worked. We asked the receptionist if we could see him, and although he was very busy, within a few minutes he had joined us. We explained Dad's situation to him and he too thought that things didn't look good in the long term without divine intervention.

Dad had quite a comfortable ride home in the ambulance, whilst we returned in the car quite depressed. This was not the news that we wanted to hear.

Our faith level seemed to be sinking a bit. Things were not happening as we thought they should, and still we had no idea why. No one seemed to think that Dad had a long-term future, and even the slightly encouraging news of the radiotherapy treatment didn't lift our spirits too much, as no assurance could be given to us that this would even work.

Later that week Irene and I called in on Dad who was now back in bed. No longer were we praying for a complete recovery. It's as if our eyes of faith could not now focus that far. We just prayed for a smaller miracle—that Dad would be able to get out of his bed and sit in a chair.

Praise God, this prayer was answered. In a few days he was able to do just that. Again our faith rose, but the battle was far from over.

Sadly the constipation problem didn't improve. With all the tablets and painkillers that he was taking there had to be some side effects I guess, so he found the regular visits by the district nurse most welcome. While the echo of our previous rejoicing was still in the air, suddenly Dad grew worse again. Mum had put a camp bed in the lounge and ingeniously put some wooden supports underneath it, as Dad was finding that the only comfortable position to be in was lying flat on his back on a firm surface.

On a Sunday night whilst my sister Heather and niece Sarah were visiting, Dad struggled to the bathroom but knew that he could only bear the pain off his bed for three minutes and then he was in real agony Ten minutes elapsed and then he returned. My sister had never seen anyone in such pain, he was sweating profusely and crying out in agony. As they prayed over him in tongues, pleading for God to remove the pain, Sarah kept feeling his pulse. The immense pain was being caused by the backbone finally giving up, and they feared another heart attack was imminent. Immediately they rang for our local doctor who came round to check things out—both our prayers and his drugs still seemed ineffective.

It was good that the doctor had chosen to visit Dad at the same time as my niece Sarah, as she was a newly qualified nurse and knew much more about what was happening than the rest of us. Our family has never been backward in coming forward and saying what we think, and Sarah was no exception. She, in her professional capacity, couldn't believe that nothing could be done to reduce the pain. She took him to one side and explained that Dad was too ill to be at home—he needed hospital treatment. On reflection I can't say that the doctor was very thrilled at being told such a commonsense thing by someone who was so much his junior, but at least he agreed to arrange an appointment for us to go and see him the following morning.

Mum, sister Heather and myself arrived punctually at the surgery the following morning, knowing that as usual the waiting room always lived up to its name to see how much patience its patients had. We gave in our name to the receptionist, and were told to take a seat and wait, and wait . . .

As I flipped through some of the tatty magazines that were piled high on the table in front of me, I wondered how many waiting suffering people would be interested in reading through this heap of outdated glossies on where you could buy a castle, or a ten-bedroomed mansion with en-suite jacuzzis in each.

Eventually the quiet waiting room emptied and we knew that it must be our turn next. The voice of the receptionist broke the long silence by informing us that the doctor was now ready to see us. So we obe-diently headed towards the door in the direction that she pointed. Our time with the doctor was brief, to put it mildly. He said that the receptionist should have told us that an ambulance was at that very moment on its way to Dad's house to take him to hospital.

That wonderful fruit of self-control stopped me

asking why we had been sitting in that miserable room fumbling through rubbish literature for all that time, when we could have been at home packing Dad's cases. I wonder why the receptionist didn't tell us—maybe she forgot!

By the time we arrived back at Dad's house the ambulance was there and as I drove up to the door I discovered my front tyre was as flat as a pancake.

Car problems always seem to come when you least need them, don't they? As I was now blocking the front door Dad had to walk slowly to the vehicle, where he very carefully climbed onto the stretcher and was strapped in. Mum jumped in and sat next to him.

As soon as I had changed my tyre, I followed the ambulance over to the hospital which was in Brighton about fifteen miles away. When I reached it, as usual, I had terrible trouble trying to find a place to park, and when I did I had even more trouble trying to find where they had put my Dad.

It was an enormous old hospital that seemed to be full of steps and long corridors. Above my head in this maze of tunnels was a low ceiling which was half hidden by ugly water pipes and sagging electrical cables. It reminded me of a trip I had recently been on to Jersey, where, in between meetings, I had been shown round one of the wartime German underground hospitals. In my view that had looked positively modern compared to this place.

After asking many people, then using the gift of a word of knowledge, I eventually found the strange little room where they had hidden Dad. There was only space for a couple of beds, a television, a wash-basin, a couple of chairs and a bookcase containing some old medical journals on cancer, which I'm sure were wonderful bedtime reading for the room's occupants.

But forgetting the surroundings, I could see that the nurses were wonderful. They could not do enough for Dad to settle him in and see that he was comfortable.

When Dad looked up and saw me, he called me over excitedly to introduce me to a gentleman who was lying in the other bed. As we shook hands I realised that Dad's next-bed-mate was in fact also a born-again Christian and a fellow elder from a church down the road from us.

Again all I thought was, 'Isn't God great! Dad is safely installed in the best place that can help him, has lovely nurses watching over him twenty-four hours a day, and is also a few feet away from fellow-shipping with a fellow suffering Christian leader.'

Mum and I returned home from the hospital knowing that God was not only still involved, but He had already been to the hospital before us to prepare the way for Dad. Although I had moaned at what I considered to be mistakes from certain doctors and receptionists, and delays in getting Dad admitted, God's timing is perfect. I knew that, Mum knew that, and my contented father knew that too.

Yes, at last we had reason to feel much more positive.

10

Laughter and Tears

When I think of hospital wards where people are seriously ill, I tend to think of them as very quiet places where the patients sleep a lot, and the only sounds to be heard are the snoring from the beds and the gentle patter of nurses' feet. It seems Dad's ward was not quite like that.

As I have mentioned, on admission Dad found that he was in the next bed to another Christian, so I know that faith-building conversation, encouragement and prayer would constantly be breaking the one-time hallowed silence.

Then it was discovered that a nurse who came from New Zealand was also a Christian. So she too had plenty to talk about with her two patients, with whom she found she had so much in common.

I could imagine that there may be times when Christians in hospital get the old Elijah feeling. Am I the only Christian in this position in the world? It's then, when you start declaring your faith, that you realise how silly that comment is. There are many Christians around that they seem to be positively crawling out from under the woodwork.

We found on our visits to Dad that he wasn't

letting the unrelenting pain get him down, which I'm sure was helped by the way the nurses were spoiling him, but even more so by the fact that he wasn't now being a burden to Mum.

One of Dad's greatest pleasures had been eating, and seeing the choice of menu that he was offered, this was one pleasure he could still enjoy whilst lying in bed within the confines of those four white walls. But sadly even this pleasure was to be short-lived. Although he enjoyed eating the food, soon afterwards his stomach rejected it and he invariably vomited it up. As the days continued, he got so fed up with being sick, he lost his desire to eat.

His friend Dick, in the next bed, was soon allowed to go home and Dad now had a very different person filling the vacant bed. This person had a foul mouth and an addiction to horse racing. This may have been a problem to many Christians, but not to Dad. For him it was yet another opportunity to share the good news of Jesus with someone who desperately needed to hear it.

Personally, I felt more sorry for our poor gambling friend in the next bed. Little did he know when he came to get treatment that he would have a Bible thumper lying right next to him commiting GBH on his ears. What made matters worse was that he wasn't even well enough to run away from Dad's enthusiastic evangelism, even if he had wanted to.

Although eating was now a problem and fasting

becoming the norm, Dad's first love was talking about Jesus. If he wasn't preaching to the guy in the next bed, he would be testifying to God's goodness to the nurses.

Of course he still liked to converse about two other things—the first being the garden. I remember him apologising to me with tears in his eyes and asking if I would forgive him for talking about gardening, but it was the one thing that kept him looking ahead to the future. This statement hit me very hard. Of course he didn't need to apologise as I was now genuinely interested in the subject—I was now a real amateur gardener and was forever after a few tips.

On one occasion his mind, which was somewhat like a gardener's calendar, seemed fixed upon onions. I guess it must have been the season for onion planting. I should mention that whenever Dad bought anything, he would always buy in bulk, and this included seeds. He always wanted to make sure that he had enough for himself and plenty to give away. He had asked my boys to divide up the hundreds of onions and put them in trays with a different member of the family's name in each tray, so they all knew which onions were theirs. We each had our allotted amount in proportion to the size of our gardens.

His other conversation topic was holidays. I had found a few days' break in my busy diary and had just bought the tickets for one of those cheap-flight, last-minute bucket deals. He was keen to listen to my plans as it always seemed to bring back happy memories of two wonderful holidays that we had spent together in Tunisia and Malta. I had also planned that we should go on a third trip overseas together, later on in May when he had got better.

Dad was also very tidy, and on each visit we had to adjust his bedside cupboard so that he could reach all the important things, like his Bible and diary, without having to lean too far, which would bring on the back pain again.

It was on Thursday 10 February that Dad got his first shock. It was 7.15 and his bedroom partner, whilst trying to make his way to the toilet, collapsed and banged his head, which caused quite a lot of bleeding. At exactly the same time a young girl also collapsed. The alarm went off as the limited number of nurses seemed to be flying everywhere, not knowing who to deal with first. The young girl staggered into Dad's room and collapsed across the now empty bed next to him.

Dad may have been sleepy but he was never too sleepy to help someone in need. He heard her mumble that she should never have come into hospital, but it was obvious that she was so ill that this was just the place that she should be.

Dad asked her name, and when she told him he told her to call upon the Lord, because he knew that He was the only one who could help her. She said that she would, and then Dad went on to tell her that the Lord has the answer to all things. She went back to her ward and Dad never saw her again.

On Friday 11 February Dad was informed that he might have to have an operation on his spine, but this would depend on the result of a scan.

I felt thrilled at this news, because for so long nothing had been done to Dad except increasing the painkillers, and I was wondering if even the doctors were losing hope and thinking that they were wasting their time.

The heavy duty drugs were now distorting Dad's vision and giving him a bad night's sleep. He would keep saying, 'The Lord said I will give you a sound mind' and he believed that He would.

When Mum and I visited on the following Monday, Dad obviously had the giggles. To start with I feared that maybe it was the effect of the drugs and that they had now decided to give him laughing gas. But then I realised it was nothing to do with chemicals—he had genuinely found something incredibly amusing!

He tried to relate to us a story of what had happened the previous day. But as he was laughing uncontrollably until the tears flowed down his cheeks, the story took a long time to unfold.

It seemed that his gambler friend, whose head was now patched up after his tumble, had been visited by his more than lively family. This included a boy and a girl.

Whilst visiting, the girl had been trying to rob the food off the patients' trolley, whilst the boy had found a video of *Jungle Book* in the rest room and was insisting that he wanted to take it home with him. The kindly nurses managed to retrieve both the food and the video after a bit of a struggle.

The curtain was then drawn around Dad's bed and the nurse gave him a bottle as he needed to pass water. Now at the best of times this sort of function demands concentration, but just as Dad was beginning to relieve himself, a head and a couple of staring eyes peered around the curtain and inquisitively asked Dad what he was doing.

As Dad related this story to us and told us of the ensuing battle that broke out as the parents tried to deal with their wayward children, he laughed so much we were frightened that he was going to have another accident. The traumas he had suffered had certainly not taken away his wonderful sense of humour, although any onlookers who didn't know him as we did may have questioned his 'sound mind'.

We left him after enjoying a very pleasant turkey sandwich in the canteen. Later that day he was told that he was to have a scan the following day. He was praising the Lord because he heard the nurse say to a doctor that he was 'urgent', and he was thinking that the sooner they got to scan him the sooner they could get to work with the surgery on his spine.

The scan however proved to be quite an experience

in itself. Thirty minutes in the tunnel scanner seemed like forever, but I know it felt great when he was able to get back into his nice warm bed, one hour and forty minutes later.

Then came the waiting period to see what the results would show. It was during this time that he lost the use of one of his legs. The doctor thought that was due to a trapped nerve.

Two days later the doctor spoke to Dad and told him that in a further two days they would operate. He explained that it was a very big operation and would take all afternoon. If all went well he should regain the use of his legs, but if it didn't go according to plan he would be in a wheelchair for the rest of his life.

When Dad told me about this I felt it looked very positive. At last they were going to do something. I had great confidence that the operation would be a success and Dad would be back on his feet again walking around in no time.

The day before the operation, Dad was told what the surgeons were planning to do. They were going to take out some of the crumbling bones in the spine and put some sort of cement between the joints. To do this they would have to cut into the left hand side of the stomach and work from there.

Dad could not move either of his legs now and although he was trusting the Lord, he broke down a few times as he considered the alternative if things didn't work out.

The thought of being a cripple for the rest of his life was something that he found very hard to cope with at this stage, but he kept trying to reassure himself that there were many people in the world who had conditions far more disabling than just the loss of the use of their legs.

After he had his heart checked, he knew he was in a spiritual war zone as he felt on top spiritually but under extreme pressure deep down. He felt that his subconscious was stirring him up, but nothing could take away the peace of Jesus from him.

He woke up on operation day feeling good and claiming that this was the day that the Lord had made; let us rejoice and be glad in it. But still the warfare raged on. Whilst these words were leaving his lips his mind was continually thinking about Mum and how she would cope if the operation failed.

It was also a big day for us at home. Hopes were high and prayers were bombarding heaven at a rate of knots. Today was the day that we were at last going to see things start to change.

11

Hope and Horror

D ad's diary—Friday 18 February.

8.30   Blood sample

9.15   Anaesthetist arrived; told me what he was
       going to do.

10.20 Given enema.

10.30 Dorothy, Heather and David came as I had to
       hang around for an hour.

11.15 Stretcher came to take me to operating
       theatre.

12.15 David spent time talking and praying with
       me until it was time to go. I had peace about
       the operation but fears about the future. I
       was moved along the draughty corridors by
       the young porters who were nice young men
       but sometimes felt they were on a race track
       bumping my toes twice. I was taken through
       a number of rooms, eventually coming along-
       side the operating table and then the anaes-
       thetist (can't spell his name) started injecting
       the arm with various needles and another

        one into the neck. They kept on prodding and talking for a long time, I had no idea until I returned to the ward.

1.30   they started—4.30 they finished.
        I woke up at 4.30 and was told the operation was unsatisfactory; they had not even started as the anaesthetist was not satisfied owing to blood clots, etc. It was a great shock going through all that to be told that the operation was a failure.

When I heard that what seemed to be the last medical hope had been abandoned I was devastated. It looked certain that Dad would never be able to walk again. My mind drifted back to the wonderful times we had spent together, and all of them seemed to hinge on the fact that God had given Dad a wonderful pair of legs that worked perfectly. I then thought how equally devastated Dad must feel. I knew that he too was putting a lot of hope in this operation. Imagine waking up thinking the operation had been completed and trying to move your legs, and then being told that it never took place, and now there was not even a fifty per cent chance that you would walk again.

That evening as I drove my Mum, sister and brother over to the hospital, they tried to put over two other more positive perspectives to me. First they explained that even if the operation had been performed, the doctors only gave Dad a fifty per cent chance of being able to walk again. They thought that maybe the Lord knew that the operation was not going to be a success, so he saved Dad all the pain plus convalescence. The other perspective was that, owing to the risk of blood clots, Dad's heart could not have coped with such a major operation, so God had actually saved Dad's life.

Although I think we were all very disappointed, we decided that however we felt, we mustn't let it show. Our job was to go and cheer Dad up.

The opposite turned out to be true. It was Dad who cheered us up, making all sorts of hilarious quips. He was wearing an oxygen mask when we arrived and at one stage he felt that Mum was talking too much, so he jokingly took it off and tried to put it over her mouth to keep her quiet. We all laughed. Although he was the first to admit he didn't know why the Lord didn't want the operation to go ahead, he was satisfied that he had committed everything to the Lord and that He was in control.

He later scribbled out these words in his diary:

On reviewing things a few days later, we can see why the operation didn't happen. We were praying that the Lord's will be done, not necessarily I should be healed. The surgeon gave me a 50/50 chance even after the op. So the Lord knew it was not time for me to go yet, and I should have. Very very seldom after making all the necessary tests is the operation stopped on the operating table.

Three days later the anaesthetist visited Dad and apologised about the operation. He explained that during those three hours, he had put Dad through various tests which all showed danger if he went ahead. Dad thanked him, but gave all credit to the Lord.

I too was now convinced that the Lord had stopped the surgeon's knife at the last minute. Had the surgeon continued, it would not just have been Dad's legs that stopped working, it would also have been his heart.

The failed operation became yet another reason to praise God.

The next few days were taken up by Dad wanting to face the future bravely. There were things he needed to sort out. Although we all agreed that there was no reason to rush into anything, there were all sorts of financial areas that needed attention. Dad could see that money was being wasted, so he cancelled his car insurance, being pretty convinced he wouldn't be driving again.

Whilst David, Tim and Mum talked through the money issues—which I must admit I did find rather tedious—my mind was busy planning how we could convert the house to make it wheelchair-friendly. I even had ideas about how he could get his chair into his beloved garden so that he would still be able to look after it.

As time had now run out for Dad's stay in this hospital, discussions were taking place about where he should go next. A nursing home was an option, but we all wanted Dad either to go to St Barnabas' for two weeks, where they would teach him how he could make the best of life without having the use of his legs, or to have him home.

This caused Dad stress because although he would have loved to come home, he again hated the thought of being a burden to Mum. The Lord solved this problem for us. St Barnabas', which because of its wonderful facilities is usually booked solid, had a bed becoming vacant in just a few days' time. So the hospital agreed to keep him with them till he could be transferred.

Meanwhile, Dad was being encouraged to do things for himself. He was given a monkey-bar attachment on his bed, which meant that he could pull himself up should he need to. He was also given a chance to sit in a chair, but this proved to be much too painful. This made Dad slightly depressed as he took it to be a personal failure. If it was possible to be healed just by your willpower and self-determination, he would have been healed months before. He was so desperate to do all he could to be well again.

The man who had trouble with his language, gambling and family had now left and yet another person was placed in the bed next to Dad's.

There were only three days to go before he would enter the wonderful environment of St Barnabas', but that night something happened that really shook Dad.

Throughout the night Dad's new arrival became delirious and got into a terrible state. He kept shouting out for Dad to help him as the nurses were trying to hurt him. Dad kept on trying to reassure him that they were only trying to help him.

It was then that Dad fell asleep, but had the most horrific dream that he had ever had. He saw the demon of death flying over him. When he awoke in a terrible state, his blood pressure had dropped, his temperature had risen, and the man who had been in the bed next to him had entered eternity.

Guilt now engrossed Dad. He blamed himself for not shouting back the way of salvation to the man who was obviously in torment.

For the next couple of days Dad was in and out of consciousness with a raging temperature and in great confusion.

David, our leader, was alongside him praying. Our church was also crying out to God for Dad's peace of mind to be restored.

Whilst all this was going on, I was leading a three-day charismatic children's leaders' conference, and it wasn't until I returned home that my family told me how bad Dad had been. They had thought he was going to die.

I have to admit that because I hadn't seen him in this condition for myself, I still did not believe that Dad was anywhere near death's door. I respected their comments, but just considered that Dad had experienced a bad turn.

As soon as I got home I went to see him, and although he wasn't eating or swallowing his tablets, he didn't look too bad to me. I guessed it was a mixture of the drugs and guilt that was pulling him down.

Anyway, I thought, tomorrow is another day. Dad will be off to St Barnabas' and this ward and the demon of death will be a thing of the past. Tomorrow is a new beginning when the recovery becomes reality and there's a chance to get him into that wheelchair and give him some independence and mobility again.

12

Devotion and Devastation

In my growing experience of hospitals I've noticed two things. The first is that nurses never change—they seem brilliant wherever they are stationed—and the second is that buildings are as different as chalk and cheese.

The part of the hospital in Brighton where Dad was, would be the sort of place that Florence Nightingale could return to and feel at home in immediately. On the other hand St Barnabas', true to the full-colour brochure, was the complete opposite.

Yes, it was tiny in comparison and privately run, but it would be great if all hospitals could be as nice. I'm convinced that just entering the light, clean and modern environment must lift the most suffering patient's spirits.

It certainly made a difference to Dad. Although he was sad to leave the wonderful nurses of Brighton, who had become very friendly with him, as soon as he entered St Barnabas' he found it uplifting.

He was put in a room with three other beds that had windows overlooking the gardens. It was light and airy, unlike the cramped space that he had been used to, where there wasn't even room to swing a cat.

Here it looked palatial, with enough room to swing a stretcher, if you needed to. Over the passageway was a large lounge which was fully equipped with comfy chairs, a sweet shop, a television and even a snooker table. Dad would really feel at home here.

On arrival Dad settled down in his new bed and was offered tea and cake. He was amazed that in the first few minutes he seemed to see more nurses than he had seen in his whole stay in Brighton. They seemed to be everywhere.

Yet another surprise was that one of the doctors had just moved up from the West Country and yes, you have guessed it, he was a Christian. I had in fact been to his church quite a few times to minister.

Dad was given a thorough examination and jokingly told not to wear tight pants. Seeing he had never worn tight pants in his life before, I hardly expected him to have the urge to now!

With the use of more drugs the pain didn't seem quite so bad, but he still couldn't move himself. Four times throughout the first night the nurses turned him.

The following day his surgical corset arrived and it was a terrible job to fit it on him. But with the aid of a special hoist even this was soon accomplished. He was also able to be hoisted gently out of the bed and lowered into a chair alongside it.

He now felt really good as he managed to sit there for an hour. Whilst there he polished off his dinner and ice cream, which at this point was fast becoming his favourite dish.

That evening I called in to see Dad and although I saw he still found it hard to swallow anything, he really looked as if he had turned a corner and was on the mend.

When he proudly told me about his hour in the chair, I again praised God and then had some prayer with him encouraging him to hang on to what God was doing. It looked as if the miracle was on its way. At this point I wasn't sure if he would be able to walk again when he came out, but I talked about getting him mobile again. I explained that if we sold his car there were amazing vehicles available for those who had lost the use of their legs. I told him that my brother Tim had even seen one arrive at the hospital where the driver couldn't use his hands or legs. We both felt excited.

After I had left, Dad started to perspire a lot, and I knew he felt exhausted. The corset and chair activities must have taken it out of him as he was still hardly eating anything.

I felt very protective towards Dad at this time, because I knew that the constant stream of visitors who understandably wanted to go and see him were also tiring him. So we made it clear to church and friends that they should not just drop in on him, but contact us first so the number could be monitored.

Dad's diary said this at the end of the day:

Very tired, but I believe in the God of the impossible, and I believe at this moment He is going to work a miracle in me. Praise the Lord.

He kept thinking of Psalm 37 verse 25. 'I have been young but now I am old and in all my years I have never seen the Lord forsake a man who loves him.'

That night he felt more movement in lifting his leg and in his toes, and he wondered what God was going to do. His last thought as he fell asleep was that a lot of the draining and exhaustion he now felt was due to showing off.

On the Wednesday I was booked to attend a leaders' conference for a couple of days, but good reports were coming back from St Barnabas'. As well as being well enough to get his hair cut, he also managed to last out one hour and thirty-five minutes in the chair on Wednesday, sit for forty-five minutes in a jacuzzi, and spend two and a half hours in the chair on the Friday.

Although this sounded like good progress, I could see that things were not quite as good as they sounded. He seemed to be spending more and more time feeling woozy and sleeping. That weekend I was off to Germany and when I mentioned to Dad the opportunities that God was giving me overseas, he seemed his old self—wide awake, alert and interested.

It was from that Friday that he could no longer manage to write his diary. Various members of the family wrote down the details of who had been to visit and how long he had been able to sit in his chair, but no longer was Dad able to write down his own personal insights and feelings.

I returned from Germany late on Sunday night, exhausted after spending many hours speaking at seminars. The news I received about Dad was not encouraging. Although he had managed to sit in his chair for three and a half hours that day, he seemed to find it hard to stay awake and concentrate for any length of time.

I felt there must be something else I should do. The miracle that both Dad and I thought we had begun to see a few days earlier, seemed to have gone into reverse.

On the Monday morning as I was praying, I felt that God guided me to pick up a book by Derek Prince called *Blessing or Curse: You Can Choose!*

I rushed over to see Dad and although he was wide awake his speech was slurred, which I assumed was the result of the drugs. I was no longer sure of anything, but if for some reason someone had managed to put a curse on Dad, I wanted us to pray against it and break its hold.

Dad as usual was more than willing to try anything. I got him to repeat after me the following words which were in the book:

Lord Jesus I believe you are the Son of God and the

only way to God and that you died on the cross for my sins and rose again from the dead. I give up all my rebellion and all my sin and I submit myself to you as my Lord. I confess all my sins before you and ask for your forgiveness, especially any sins that exposed me to a curse. Release me from the consequences of my ancestors' sins. By decision of my will I forgive all who have harmed me or wronged me, just as I want God to forgive me. I cancel all Satan's claims against me. Lord Jesus I believe that on the cross you took on yourself every curse that could ever come upon me. So I ask you now to release me from every curse over my life. In your name Lord Jesus Christ. By faith I now receive my release and thank you for it.

Dad stumbled over a few of the words so I went over them again to make sure that he had repeated accurately everything that I had said.

We felt good. We felt that any curse that may have been upon Dad's life would now have been lifted. This must be the start of his health returning because I could not think of anything else that we needed to do or needed to pray. Now it really was up to the Lord. Dad was in His hands and believing for a healing.

Later that evening I returned with the prayer that Dad had prayed typed out, and I stuck it to the cupboard next to his bed so that he could easily see it and be reminded that victory was on the way. I was thrilled to see him eating his tea. Surely that must be a good sign.

It was just a few days before we were due to go on holiday, so Irene and I went to see the doctor to find out how Dad was progressing. Dad was aware that we had an interview, but was not sure when. Whilst the rest of the family went to sit with Dad, Irene and I secretly made our way to the doctor's office. I guessed deep down that we might hear some bad news and I did not wish to be quizzed by Dad afterwards, as the medical facts may have brought about depression and made him lose faith in his healing.

After the doctor sat us down, he gently but honestly said everything that I did not want to hear.

The spine had collapsed, which had practically made the kidneys useless. So Dad's body was slowly being poisoned. For the first time it hit me that my father was dying. I asked how long he had, and should we go on holiday. The doctor found this very hard to answer, but he didn't think Dad was likely to deteriorate that quickly.

This was the saddest day of my life.

My faith in Dad being healed was gone.

When we went to join Dad and the family, I felt his eyes kept staring at me and I could not stop the tears from rolling down my cheeks. I have never felt this way before.

As soon as was convenient I made an excuse about having to leave, and after I had gone Dad told Mum that I had been crying. He must have guessed something was terribly wrong because he hadn't seen me cry since I was a child. He then went on to say five words that will remain with me for the rest of my life. 'It hasn't worked, has it?' Some of my family thought that he may have been referring to the hospital treatment, but I knew he could only be thinking of one thing, my prayer . . . everyone went silent when he said this. There was no answer that anyone could give him.

13

Life and Death

As I returned home, devastated, Irene poured me a drop of brandy. As I sipped it I recollected how much I enjoyed a glass of brandy after a good meal, but now this tasted bitter. David also joined us and both of them prayed for me.

Throughout the afternoon I managed to compose myself. Whilst Dad was still alive there was still hope. I was not going to give up praying for his healing. I returned to see him in the evening. It was easy to see that everything had changed. Dad prayed over each member of the family, which was like a re-run from the Old Testament where the dying father would give his blessings to his children. Then he ordered a double portion of ice cream, which was now practically the only food he was able to eat. He asked me when I was due to leave for my holiday, and I told him tomorrow at 8 a.m.

Things were made worse by the man in the next bed. He looked quite fit and was even able to move around, but his family must have also been told some sad news because they too were in tears. As the distressed wife left she reminded him that she was keeping the bed warm for him; but seeing this distraught family was reminding us of Dad's short future. Just as laughter encourages laughter, so tears encourage tears.

The man in the next bed died that very night, which I am sure that Dad would have noticed.

As I returned home, my mind was now in turmoil over the silly holiday. If I went it would be a total disaster because I would be wondering how Dad was every minute of every day. Yet if I stayed, and went and saw Dad tomorrow when he knew I should be on a plane, would he think that I had given up believing that he could be made well, and was I just hanging around knowing that his time was short? After good advice from loved ones, I cancelled the holiday, and I praise the Lord that I did.

The following morning I made my usual daily trip to Mum's house, and just as I should have been flying out of Gatwick, the hospice phoned to say that Dad had taken a turn for the worse. Neither Mum nor I could control ourselves. We just burst into tears. I said I would ring round the family and get them to come here, then we could all go over together. I got to the phone and broke down again. I couldn't bring myself to tell anyone that Dad was dying. When the family arrived we all wept together. This was the first time in living memory that this had happened.

It was a grey miserable day, which summed up how

we were feeling. We went to St Barnabas' and Dad was now unconscious. We were told that the hearing was the last faculty to go, so we talked to Dad and prayed over him, realising that he was not going to talk back.

As I left the building I made up my mind that I would not enter it again. I could not face seeing him lying there deteriorating with the thought of him being taken from me. I wanted to remember him how he was, not as I saw him now.

I arrived home to find that a copy of my new recently recorded cassette had arrived. I didn't even want to hear it.

That night, despite all I had said, I went back to spend a few hours at Dad's side. I took my new cassette, plus a player and headphones, which I gently put over his head. I told him that I wouldn't let him go without hearing my latest album. I think he enjoyed it.

Afterwards I just sat and looked at him. It made no difference if I cried or not now, as he was no longer opening his eyes. He still looked so well and in such good shape. His beautiful skin looked as good as it always had and his cheeks had lost none of their rosy complexion. I still couldn't believe that he was dying. I half expected him to suddenly sit up smiling and say that he was only kidding.

He had times when he made noises and sounded restless, but I was unsure if that was due to pain in his body, thoughts in his mind, or maybe he was just trying to answer me.

Thursday was a lovely bright sunny day, but as Irene joined me to sit with him throughout the evening, we discovered that although the sky was very clear the temperature was icy cold.

Again we talked to Dad and read him Scripture, and I was still praying like mad that he would show some sign of a miraculous recovery. I whispered into his ear some words that I imagine Jesus would have said to a dying man, but the difference was that when Jesus spoke the sick person always leapt to their feet healed. When I spoke my Dad just continued to lie there.

On Friday 11 March the sun was shining down from a beautiful blue sky that was patterned with fluffy clouds. The ground was white, carpeted with a heavy frost.

Dad, who was now in a room by himself, had not changed for better or for worse in the last forty-eight hours. It was just before 1.50 p.m., and the family had been waiting in the lounge for the nurses to turn him, when they called us back in. Within seconds Dad sort of opened his eyes for his last look round, made a sound from his throat, and then a nurse touched his pulse and informed us he had gone.

Immediately, as his heart stopped pumping, those rosy cheeks went white, as did the rest of his body, and we all knew that we were no longer looking at Dad. He was no longer here.

As we all wept uncontrollably, I discreetly took the prayer of victory off the cupboard door, and screwed it up as I put it in my pocket.

14

Tragedy and Triumph

All readers who have lost a loved one will under stand what I mean when I say I felt gutted and empty.

I didn't know what was going on, what had gone wrong. I didn't want to think about anything. I had not just lost my father, I had lost one of my closest friends. I felt life had lost its relevance. I was aching inside with an emotion that I had never experienced before and I didn't know how to cope with it.

I have always taken my responsibilities very seriously. Here I was, a church leader, who had become a friend and influence to many thousands of children and adults throughout the world. Would I ever have anything to offer them again? I had to find what I had lost.

Something in me said that I needed to go and find Dad, then hopefully that would get my mind sorted out. Where could I find him? I knew where his white shell was, but, I repeat, that was no longer my Dad.

As we were due to be abroad I had no engagements that weekend, so it gave me the opportunity to take forty-eight hours' drive and see what I could find. Irene of course came with me.

Some may say that I was running away from reality and responsibility, but neither of these were true. For me it was a chance to spend an uninterrupted time with my Heavenly Father so that I could get the right perspectives on my earthly father.

I drove to Dad's favourite holiday resorts and retraced his footsteps in the West Country. Walking along the Cobb at Lyme Regis, at times I thought I could see him swinging his walking stick as he strode along the seafront with his green haversack over his shoulder.

Then we climbed a hill called Golden Cap, which was situated right next door to his favourite caravan site. As I reached the top of the hill I could imagine him with his brown corduroy hat on, gazing out to sea through his binoculars.

But these memories were not tearful ones. These were happy ones. God has allowed me a very vivid imagination, and I knew the only way to get my dying father out of my mind was to envisage my living father in the places he loved the most.

I think some people thought I was crazy to make such a trip, but as I returned home I knew I had done the right thing.

I also found it fascinating how a bereavement can change your enemies' attitude to you. Let me explain. Along with many others in our church, I am a member of our local village sports and social club. It's

where a close-knit community of local people gather
to have a chat and a beer.

I too love having a chat and a beer, as do many
other Christians. I have never hidden the fact that I
am a Christian; I've even put my name under
'Reverend' in the members' book.

The vast majority of the locals seemed to like us
because they have discovered that Christians are nice
people who don't get drunk, swear all the time or
hypocritically act out being 'holier than thou'. They
have discovered to their surprise that a Christian just
gets quietly on with living out his faith, but is always
looking for the opportunity to share it with anyone
who is interested.

But then, in this setting, you will always get the one
or two who are maybe outright atheists, people with
guilt, or backsliders. These tend to go the other way
and openly mock us. I've had a couple of people who
gave me my fair share of verbal persecution!

The night I returned home I dropped in for a pint,
and not only did the head barman walk over and put
his arm consolingly around me, but the ones that had
previously given me all the aggression, suddenly made
friends and have remained so.

Thank you Lord for the love and care that you put
into those who are not yet yours—the next step is to
see them saved.

The days dragged by as we were all waiting for the

funeral service and wondering how we were going to cope in public. The church was also grieving, as the leaders broke down in tears at the front of the meetings. It was wonderful to see how much Dad had been loved and respected.

I walked around with dark glasses on, as the slightest sight or even smell that brought back memories of Dad, also brought tears to my eyes. I told myself I could never go in his wonderful garden again; but then thinking he would never forgive me if I didn't see to those stupid onions, I had to go round and plant them. It was true—onions do make you cry. The amount of water they received should make them grow up to be champions. Irene was very protective towards me during this time. She knew that I didn't know what I was doing half the time, and would not let me drive out without coming with me.

I bought four pretty little trees for each family to plant in their gardens to remind us of Dad. Much better I thought than some grey tombstone.

The funeral went well. I personally found it more emotional walking around a garden centre than I did meeting in a religious building, because I just could not imagine Dad in a building like this. (Our church has always met in village halls and schools.)

Later we held a memorial service, which was packed with Dad's friends. It was a great time. We didn't bother to sing anything, as Dad never did have the sweetest of voices and was never that much into singing. So we thought that to honour him we would give it a miss.

Then it was business as usual. Spring Harvest for four weeks, a return to America, as well as getting back to see what God wanted to continue doing in our local church. Being busy was marvellous because it didn't leave me time to think about what had happened.

Although I've mentioned a lot about my own feelings, of course after Dad's death Mum suffered more than anyone.

It must be strange walking in the same garden, living in the same house, sleeping in the same bed, without the loved one who has shared all those things with you for the past fifty years. She told me that the hardest thing to come to terms with was that since their wedding vows she had promised to obey Dad as the head of the household. It's hard when the head is taken away, and now she had to take over that role and make decisions that she had previously handed over to Dad to make.

Although she is coping very well, and has even taken up the gardening, I know that the nights are long and lonely, holidays will never be the same, and she feels an odd one out even when she spends time with married couples that she knows well.

I know that she's grateful that she still has the Lord

Jesus, her strong faith, and a church that loves her. But will there ever be a day when any of these can fill the hole in her life that Dad has left?

The family try to spend as much time with her as possible, but now she has a lot of free time and we seem to have so little, even that can be a strain.

So here I am, nearly five months after Dad went to be with the Lord, and I am no longer questioning that it was the right time for Dad to die. I know that God's timing was perfect—it's mine that wasn't. He allowed us to have Dad for those extra years that we asked for after his heart attack, but I wonder if even that was a selfish prayer, and if he had gone and been with the Lord then, he would not have had any of the last two years of suffering to endure.

I still have many questions such as, 'Why did he have to go through so much pain when he had so much prayer?' Also, when the doctor gave me the facts, I crumbled. Would it have made any difference if I had stayed strong in faith? Maybe by the time I meet the only person who can give me the answers, I won't be too worried about them, because I'll also be reunited with my wonderful Dad again, and he certainly won't be thinking anything about pain and tears.

Am I any different now than I was five months ago? Most definitely. I am much more emotional. I tend to be a little more serious. I find I can really mourn now with those who are mourning, and I feel I have a gap in my life the size of my father. I miss him like crazy.

No one can take his place, and for the rest of my life there will be occasions, objects and places that will remind me of him, and I know I will need to put the dark glasses on to cover my grief.

Dad blessed many people when he was alive. The greatest way that he would want me to honour him is to be even more zealous for Jesus, and that is what I intend to be.

Have I given up on healing? Most certainly not. I must confess that my faith in healing was at times shaken, and I did need my brothers' and sisters' prayers to help me get back to where I should be. But now, thanks to Jesus, I have learned so much from my father's life and death that I feel more in faith for God to do the miraculous, than I have done at any stage of my Christian life.

I try to pray for those who are sick at any opportunity I can. Sure, if I am honest, there is still a lot I don't understand about it, but Jesus hasn't told me to understand it, He has just told me to do it.

Over the past few months the church, the family and I have received an amazing fresh anointing from God. People started not to worry about image when Dad died, and they freely let their emotions show. Now the Holy Spirit has breathed anew upon us, and we are not worried about looking foolish in public. I have come to a new realisation that I am empty and can do nothing, but when I am full of the Holy Spirit with Jesus' help I can do anything.

Finally, here's some advice to those who still have parents alive whom they love.

1. Don't be frightened to both tell them and show them how much they mean to you.

2. Spend as much time as you can with them because even if they don't look it, they are getting older, and no one knows God's timing for their lives on earth.

3. Show an interest in them. Don't spend all your time talking about yourself or your children.

4. You don't always have to agree with them, but the Bible says that we should honour and respect them.

5. Don't leave them out. Invite them to meals, take them on trips, even take them on holiday with you—and take plenty of photographs.

6. Show an interest in their interests, because if you ever reach their age, there is a good chance they will also be your interests.

7. Pray with them regularly, and also share with each other what you have learned from Scripture.

8. Let your own children see how much you love, care for, and respect your parents. Then maybe one day they will do the same for you.

They will pass on and probably before you do; but at least like me you'll have great memories of the time the Lord allowed you to spend together whilst you were on earth. And loving memories never die, they only grow stronger.

In the Hands of the Potter

Dale Evans Rogers

*Have you ever felt your world was collapsing,
but you were able to put on such a good act
that no one could see it?*

In 1948 Dale Evans Rogers seemed to have everything: a successful career as a film star, a new marriage to Roy Rogers, and an adorable family. The future couldn't have looked brighter, but, as she says, 'What I didn't know was that the Master Potter was about to begin shaping my life in very painful ways.'

Using the analogy of the potter and the clay, she traces God's handiwork in her life from her youthful rebellion, to her success as a Hollywood celebrity, to her joys and sorrows as a wife and mother.

Through career crises, the birth of a child with Down's syndrome, the deaths of three beloved children and severe health problems, she found that God was using adversity to create beauty in her life. She learned to allow Him to be in control, and what could have been a tale of tragedy became a story of triumph.

Catalogue Number YB 4030   £4.99

Why Grace Changes Everything

Chuck Smith

Grace—it's a word we all love to hear. But how many people really know what it means? Without it our lives are dry and dusty. But when grace comes, it transforms our lives into something rich and beautiful. With the passion of a man whose own life has been transformed by this gift, Chuck Smith clearly explains why:

- We are not bound to God by a huge list of *do's* and *don'ts*.
- Our mistakes will never alienate us from God.
- There is only *one* thing we can do to please God.
- Our relationship with God does not depend on our efforts, but on His unchanging and loving character.

Discover why grace makes life worth living!

Catalogue Number YB 4034 £4.99

The Life God Blesses

Gordon MacDonald

Are You Prepared for the Storms of Life?

Gliding along the sometimes rough, sometimes tranquil, mostly invigorating seas, we often set out on life's voyage with little regard to the quality of our vessel. We are more concerned with our ship's appearance than with what lies below the waterline—the all-important soul that acts as a keel to keep us afloat should the waters turn tempestuous.

In this gracefully written book, Gordon MacDonald navigates seldom charted depths and steers us towards the disciplines, convictions, silence, beauty and spirit that feed and prepare the soul to recognise and receive God's blessings.

Catalogue Number YB 4031   £4.99

Hope for the Troubled Heart

Billy Graham

As no other author can, Billy Graham answers the questions plaguing humanity today with boldness and compassion.

- A man laid off just before retirement
- Parents whose home is a war zone
- A mother whose child is ravaged by drugs
- An affluent entrepreneur who cannot shake life's emptiness
- A parent whose only son died in the Gulf War

Sooner or later all of us experience pain and frustration from the times we live in. That's why Dr Billy Graham has written this new book, drawing on the accumulated wisdom and experience of a lifetime of ministry, and illustrating his points with examples of very *present-day* hurts and how people have coped with them.

With *Hope for the Troubled Heart*, you can:

- Grasp the depth of God's love in the midst of your personal hurts.
- Face failure and disillusionment realistically, but with unshakeable hope.
- Learn to pray through your pain and confidence.
- Store up strength for the storms on the horizon.
- Look at life as the training ground for heaven.

In what could be considered the culmination of his worldwide ministry, Dr Graham shows us how to live day by day in the real world, even though it is filled with pain. And he gives us the hope to survive and triumph in the uncertain years to come.

Catalogue Number YB 9530   £3.99

When Heaven is Silent

Ronald Dunn

'Jesus refused to answer the "why" of suffering because the ultimate issue is how we are to respond to that suffering. "Why me?" solves nothing. Only when we face up to the inadequacy of this question will we be free to ask the right one, the one put forth by Christ Himself, "What now?" This question transforms the landscape of suffering from a random, accidental absurdity to a vital part of the grand scheme of a great God.'

Ronald Dunn

The author's personal experiences of tragedy and depression are woven into his detailed studies of Jacob's wrestling with the angel, Job's catalogue of sufferings, King David's disappointments and the 'dark night of the soul' expressed in his Psalms. He also considers Jesus' encounter with the man born blind, Joseph's treatment at the hands of his brothers and that most unbelievable verse, Romans 8:28. He agonises over the way good and evil are inextricably mixed up in our lives, how we often struggle 'until the breaking of the day' against what are in fact our blessings, and bring darkness on ourselves by failing to persevere.

Ronald Dunn came through his darkness and can assure his readers that such periods are inevitable for every believer, that we have the right to cry out in pain as Jesus did on the cross—and the Church should recognise this, not condemn it—and that though we flee God, He will not abandon us and truly does cause 'all things to work together for good to those who love Him . . . who are called according to His purpose.'

Catalogue Number YB 9642   £4.50